The Virgin
Baby Names

Jane Spence

Virgin

For Carol Diana Patricia,
Francis Maxwell, Justin, Ka,
Gisela, Sebastian and Bruno

*

And for baby Adriana Dominique,
may she never shed a Tia!

First published in Great Britain 1993 by
Virgin Books
an imprint of Virgin Publishing Ltd
332 Ladbroke Grove
London W10 5AH

Reprinted 1995, 1997

A catalogue record of this title is available from the British
Library

ISBN 0 86369 641 4

Typeset by Phoenix Photosetting, Chatham, Kent.
Printed and bound in Great Britain by
Cox & Wyman Ltd, Reading, Berkshire.

Contents

Introduction   v

From Britannia to Hollywood: A brief history
 of names   1

Pitfalls and Problems: Ten traps to avoid   21

Suffer the Little Children: Baptism   27

Naming Names: From registration to deed poll   31

Stylefile: Coming or going?   35

Image: Selling your baby!   67

Wannabees: Babes on top   83

Sex: From Rambo to Bimbo   91

Time and Space: Naming the day   107

Literary Allusions: Literary illusions and poetic
 fallacies   121

Glossary of Girls' Names   133

Glossary of Boys' Names   183

Introduction

New horizons have opened, full of Nineties names which truly reflect life today – names which say something about us, about our style, our values and our ambitions, about our sense of the world and its cultures, about our sense of the past and our sense of that strange, wonderful future which beckons to our babies.

Divided into Style, Image and Sex, this book is the DIY guide to finding a really sharp name for Millennial Baby. It will introduce you to Whizz Kids and Was Kids, tell you how to avoid getting a Rambo, a Bimbo, or a Wimp, tell you how to beat the crush and go for originality, or how to start a trend if you're set on fashionability. At the back is a comprehensive glossary of names and their meanings to help you make the momentous decision of naming your child. For the aim of this book is to take the post-natal depression out of choosing a name. The thing should be fun. After all, it's your baby. Why not enjoy it?

What's In a Name?

Adam and Eve didn't hang about when it came to going forth and multiplying. Once they'd got the knack, it was easy. Thanks to their indecent enthusiasm for the job, there are more people alive today than have died in the whole history of the human race. Small wonder that parents seek original names to give their children some individuality in the global sardine tin that has become our home. There's not much room at the top – so if we can crown our babies with early distinction, so much the better.

In some cultures, children are not considered born until they have been named. Britain's system of birth registration is a bureaucratic form of the same belief. Society is a club and your name is the entrance fee exacted for membership. Once you've got a name, you're in for life. Your first name denotes your status as a person while your surname portrays your group affiliations within the whole. The compound of both is what we regard as *you*. And although you can 'change' your name for practical purposes, what's on your actual birth certificate stays; to society, you are, and will always remain, what you were when you first joined the club.

Names convey far richer information than a number could. Take houses, for example. What does Number 33 tell you? Not much. But with names, it's different. They define our whole existence in society's status quo.

Having a word for something gives you power over it. That's the essence of language. And having names for people, knowing who and what and where they are is the essence of social control. In Genesis, Yahweh gives Adam dominion over the animals and over Eve by letting him name them. But He keeps His own omnipotence secure by having a name too sacred to be spoken. Like Yahweh, members of many tribal communities won't tell you their names, fearing that this intimate knowledge will give you power over them, for they regard names not as external tags, but as the very handles of the soul.

Some people, such as nuns and monks, abandon their personal names, as do actors and singers, although for very different reasons. For most people, however, names are a label for life, lovingly picked by parents who hope their choice will suit the blank, mysterious personality of each baby. And it's a big responsibility, for what goes on your birth certificate goes also on your school books, your passport, your CV; it goes on the death certificate and on the tombstone. Your name *is* your identity, the outward expression of your individuality, the public part of your secret self. And letting someone call you by your first name, although quite common in these informal days, is nonetheless a gesture of opening. Like inviting a stranger into your home, it gives intimacy an entrée and a seat at the hearth.

A rose by any other name might smell as sweet, but is that really true of people, with their rich suggestive psyches? We grow like our names as we grow like our dogs – and in the eyes of society, we are what we're called, just as we are what we eat. So get it right and, while your babies may have a lot to live up to, they will do so with flying colours and grow into those very special and lovely gifts, their names.

From Britannia to Hollywood

A brief history of names

Latin Names: *The Britons Go Roman*

Way back when the true-blue Brits were still romping around in woad, there wasn't a Wendy in sight. Although Boudicca wore the pants and the men wore plaits, the Celts didn't muck about when it came to names. They liked no-fuss one-thought punch-lines that reflected a personal attribute, like Big Ears, say, or Extremely-Tall-Person-In-Socks. Hence, you might be known as Caratacos, 'amiable', Artos, 'bear-like', or Cunovals, 'high'n'-'mighty'. Under the Celtic system, names described the person but not his place or role in society.

Great fireside drinkers and boasters, the Celtic tribesmen liked to make a big song and dance about their prowess as warriors. In fact, they were peaceable hicks and, when the Romans arrived in 43 BC, the clodhoppers in their carts proved to be no match for the newcomers.

Grumbling but acquiescent, they succumbed to occupation and became Romano-Britons. Over the years, many even adopted the Latin three-fold name describing an individual's family, tribe, and the personal nickname by which he was commonly known. The famous lawyer and statesman Marcus Tullius Cicero, for example, was simply called Cicero, meaning 'chickpea'. If we were to apply the same system nowadays, a modern Roman-by-any-other-name might be 'Carter Georgia Peanuts'.

Although the Romans stayed on the island they called Britannia for some five hundred years, when they finally left their influence did not last and neither did their names. The odd name survived in the Welsh outback – Emlyn is often cited as a corruption of Aemilianus, Kay and Cai as vestiges of Caius – but when the body of Britannia fell to Anglo-Saxon marauders in their Black Forest bateaux, Romano-British nomenclature passed forever into the Dark Age and was rapidly forgotten.

ROMAN GIRLS	ROMAN BOYS
Aemilia	Augustus
Augusta	Aurelius
Aurelia	Brutus
Calpurnia	Caius
Claudia	Cassius
Clodia	Claudius
Cornelia	Cornelius
Drusilla	Fabius
Flavia	Faustus
Julia	Felix
Justina	Gaius
Livia	Hadrian
Lucilla	Julius
Lucretia	Lucius
Marcella	Magnus
Petronella	Marcus
Priscilla	Marius
Virginia	Titus

Anglo-Saxon Names: *The Hyphen Cometh*

The Anglo-Saxons, who could do two things at once, like thinking and talking, imported twin-idea names such as Ethel-red, meaning 'noble-counsel', and Alfred, meaning 'elf-counsel'. Called 'Engles', these double-barrelled, two-fisted tribes muscled into Britain from Germany and central Europe and settled there with all their friends and relations. Britain went German – in one fell swoop, Britannia became Englaland, 'the land of the Engles and Schleswig'. The Engle lingo, Englisc, was what we now call Old English. It was rooted in the mother tongue of the Vaterland which the occupying Engelberts had left behind; Old English was the doppelganger of Old German. This meant that when Britain was later invaded by the Scandinavian scavengers of the eighth century, although Vikings and their victims didn't see eye to eye, they could at least call each other names.

OLD ENGLISHWOMEN	OLD ENGLISHMEN
Aldith	Alaric
Audrey	Aldhelm
Brenda	Aldred
Edith	Aldwin
Elfreda	Alfred
Elgiva	Alwyn
Estrild	Amfrid
Ethel	Brand
Ethelfleda	Canute
Ethelinda	Cerdic
Fredegonde	Cuthbert
Frideswide	Dunstan
Gertrudis	Edgar
Godiva	Edmund
Gunilda	Edred
Gunnora	Edwin
Hilda	Godwin
Ingrid	Hereward
Rowena	Osgar
Sigrid	Randal
	Ranulf
	Siward
	Thorkell

- 'Ethel' may not sound glamorous nowadays, but it means 'noble' and was the Old English prefix reserved for names denoting those with royal blood.

Early Christian Names: *Pilgrim's Progress*

In AD 597 St Augustine and thirty godsbodies arrived in Britain, charged by Pope Gregory with converting the Engles to Christianity. King Ethelbert of Kent let the do-gooders build an Englican church in Canterbury and allowed Augustine to baptise him into the strange new faith. Christianity became fashionable and Anglo-Saxon Kent quickly followed the trend. Christianity took many years to spread beyond Kent, however, and initially only priests and nuns adopted saints' names in the early days of a process which would later come to dominate naming as the Church gathered strength.

EARLY CHRISTIAN MOTHERS	EARLY CHRISTIAN FATHERS
Albina	Aidan
Alburga	Alard
Barbara	Alban
Edburga	Aldous
Hildegard	Alphege
Juliana	Ambrose
Juliot	Anselm
Mildred	Bede
Radegunde	Botolph
Urith	Jacob
Ursula	Swithin
Winifred	Thurstan

Norman Names: *Fallen Angles*

When it came to battle, Angles on horseback felt unsafe. As a result, they preferred to fight on foot. At Hastings, Harold's infantry couldn't stand up to the Norman cavalry – and William's mounties rode roughshod over the Anglo-Saxons. It was the beginning of civilisation as we know it. Once they had poked Harold in the eye and littered Hastings with the luminaries of Saxon society, the stormin' Normans set about destroying the culture they had conquered, humiliating its ruling class, and abolishing Englisc as the language of Top People. The new bosses spoke French and wrote Latin. Although the Normans were themselves of Norse blood and their original Old German names had Old English counterparts, these became gallicised and latinised into the names which are still familiar today.

NORMAN GIRLS	NORMAN BOYS
Agnes	Algernon
Avice	Archibald
Bertha	Augustine
Cecily	Baldric
Cicely	Bardolph
Elena	Barret
Ella	Bartholomew
	Benedict

NORMAN GIRLS	NORMAN BOYS	
Emma	Bernard	Humphrey
Emmeline	Bertram	Ivo
Gisela	Bevis	Jocelyn
Heloise	Brian	Luke
Ida	Durrant	Matthew
Margaret	Emery	Maurice
Matilda	Eustace	Maynard
Maude	Fulke	Miles
Oriel	Geoffrey	Neville
Rosamund	Gerald	Odo
	Gerard	Oliver
	Gervase	Ralph
	Gilbert	Reynard
	Godfrey	Richard
	Gregory	Robert
	Guy	Roger
	Harvey	Roland
	Henry	Rolf
	Herbert	Rollo
	Herman	Walter
	Hugo	William

- Algernon means 'whiskery' and began as a nickname for one of William the Conqueror's chums who was a bit hairy for the clean-shaven Normans. Other hair pieces: Crispin means 'curly' and Calvin means 'bald' and Brendan means 'stinking hair'.

Saintly Names: *Britain Goes Catholic*

Mother Church had long exhorted her flock to name new babies after angels and saints. But the Flock did what it liked. However, by the twelfth century the Church had become exceedingly powerful and was able to exert God's will in no uncertain terms. The Flock knew when it was beaten and obediently began taking what we now call Christian names. In trotted an apostolic succession of Peters, followed by Lukes and Philips. Hard on their heels came the names of holy women. Agneses, Annes, Elizabeths, and Joans appeared as ewers hit basins with an Almighty splash. Later Mother Church tightened her grip when the Council of Trent (1545–63) decreed that baptismal names *had* to be drawn from the New Testament and the calendar of saints. Chaos ensued. As the Flock grew bigger, more and more sheep were dipped under the same few Christian names, causing a massive Identity Crisis. Nobody knew who anybody was, even people who were Somebody. Thus surnames – like London, Smith, or Jackson – gradually evolved, pinning down myriad Matthews, Marks, Lukes and Johns by place, profession, and paternity.

SAINTLY GIRLS	SAINTLY BOYS	
Agnes	Aidan	James
Anne	Alban	Jerome
Beatrice	Aldhelm	John
Catherine	Andrew	Joseph
Denise	Anselm	Laurence
Elizabeth	Antony	Leonard
Isabel	Augustine	Luke
Joan	Barnabas	Mark
Katharine	Bartholomew	Matthew
Magdalen	Basil	Michael
Mary	Bede	Nicholas
	Benedict	Paul
	Bernard	Peter
	Cyprian	Philip
	Cyril	Simon
	Daniel	Theodore
	Denis	Thomas
	Dunstan	Timothy
	Egbert	

SWOT-SPOT

- Despite the best efforts of the Church, the most
  frequently given first name today is that of Mohammed,
  the prophet who founded the religion of Islam.

Old Testament Names: *Britain Goes Protestant*

Name-dropping took a fresh twist during the Reformation. When Tudor England split from Rome, the names of saints and martyrs bit the dust as Protestants cast down everything that smacked of popery. All non-scriptural saints fell into disfavour. Even the New Testament itself was regarded with distrust. With the strengthening of the breakaway religion, however, came publication of the first English Bible, and Protestant mums-to-be began trawling happily through the Old Testament for names to replace those of the defrocked Catholic calendar. From Zedekiah to Ezekiel, the anti-clerical went in pursuit of the unspellable, producing the unspeakable on the way.

BIBLICAL GIRLS	BIBLICAL BOYS
Abigail	Abel
Bathsheba	Absalom
Delilah	Ebenezer
Elisheva	Enoch
Hadassah	Jedediah
Zipporah	Obadiah

SWOT-SPOT

* There are 3,037 male names in the Bible and only 81 female names.

Puritan Names: *The Importance of Being Earnest*

If the Protestants thought they were better than the Papists, then the Puritans thought they were better than everyone, with the doubtful exception of God. They were holier-than-thou, and said so in fire'n'brimstone. They searched low and lower for the humblest possible names with which to belittle their babies, but since most of the OT names had already been pinched by the Protestants, the Glums had to go one worse. They invented their own names which bore horrible moral messages and were hung like tombstones around the necks of the newborn. Dust, Ashes, and Tribulation rubbed shoulders with No-Merit and More Triall. There was even a Preserved Fish. But the weirdest was poor little If-Jesus-Christ-Had-Not-Died-For-Thee-Thou-Hadst-Been-Damned Barebones. In later life, this terrible infant changed his name to Nicholas Barbon. After such a mouthful, most would have turned to Bourbon.

PURITAN GIRLS	PURITAN BOYS
Discipline	Donatas
Earth	Praise-God
Livewell	Repentance
Reformation	Sorry-for-Sin

SWOT-SPOT

- The sixteenth-century minister Thomas Heley called his four children Much-Merceye, Increased, Sin-denie and Fear-not.

Georgian Names: *Pompous and Circumstanza*

When Queen Anne popped her clogs in 1714, the British crown passed to the Hanoverians, who imported high-sounding names with a hint of imperial Rome. Austere and commanding, Augustas looked down their Roman noses at Georgianas while Amelias, Adolphas, and Sophias glimmered statuesquely through the social columns. The pomposity was international: 'a' and 'us' divided Them from Us. But not for long. The classes eager to clamber up the social ladder gave their children all sorts of aspirant appellations. Social climbing had arrived.

GEORGIAN GIRLS	GEORGIAN BOYS
Albina	Adolphus
Anastasia	Augustus
Arabella	Aurelius
Aurelia	Gustavus
Carola	Octavius
Clarinda	Ostorius
Claudia	Postumus
Davina	Septimus
Frederica	Theophilus
Laetitia	Titus
Lavinia	
Louisa	
Richenda	
Theophila	
Wilhelmina	

SWOT-SPOT

- In 1781, a Wiltshire tailor christened his son Charles Caractacus Ostorius Maximilian Gustavus Adolphus Stone.
- Goldsmith invented a character called Miss Carolina Wilhelmina Amelia Skeggs, to poke fun at the pretentious naming of this time.

Romantic and Pre-Raphaelite Names: *Britain Goes Gothic*

When they weren't painting the map pink, the Victorians were suckers for romance and anything savouring of the Gothic. With many a backward glance, they dreamed knightly of Shalott, Camelot, Lancelot and every other Celt-belt hot-shot trotted out by Walter Scott. The potent influence of his novels revived names like Wilfred and Roland; even Guy – held nervously at arm's length since the Gunpowder Plot – was allowed back into the drawing-room under Scott's patronage, just as Maud, under Tennyson's came into common (or garden) usage while the Pre-Raphs swooned over Mabel and Edith, their unlikely favourites. Anything Saxon was quite the thing; Edgars and Alfreds crowded fashionably in from the obscurity in which they had lain for centuries. And what the Romantic Movement did through literature, the Oxford Movement did through liturgy. Committed to beefing up the credibility of the Anglican Church, the so-called Tractarians dusted down the fallen saints and replaced them on their pedestals, haloes intact.

ROMANTIC GIRLS	ROMANTIC BOYS
Amabel	Alfred
Amy	Athelstan
Eglentyne	Edgar
Elfleda	Edred
Emma	Edwin
Matilda	Ethelred
	Galfrid
	Guy
	Quentin
	Roland
	Wilfrid

PRE-RAPH GIRLS	PRE-RAPH BOYS
Alice	Aylmer
Edith	Galahad
Elaine	Gareth
Ella	Geraint
Enid	Hugh
Mabel	Lancelot
Maud	Ralph
	Roger
	Walter

Surnames as First Names: *Famous Last Words*

During the nineteenth century, many parents began christening children with a surname, particularly that of the mother's family. Last names started to come first and soon Ross, Scott, Fraser and Glen were acceptable 'Christian' names. Another Victorian fashion was the rather snobbish misappropriation of aristocratic surnames for use as first names by commoners, most of whom could claim not the slightest connection with the nobility concerned.

NOBLE NAMES GONE CHRISTIAN

Courtenay	Percy
Douglas	Russell
Dudley	Sidney
Gordon	Spencer
Greville	Stuart
Howard	Talbot
Neville	Wallace
Pelham	Windsor

SWOT-SPOT

- The name Clive was introduced in the eighteenth century by members of the East India Company who wanted to honour Robert Clive (1725–74), the soldier and statesman known as Clive of India.

Post-War Names: *Citizens of the World*

Two world wars and a century of tremendous migration have flung cultures together, mixing up New World with Old, spicing the language that Shakespeare spoke with Spanish, Italian, German, Yiddish, Arabic and the rhythms of Black and Indian speech. Fed by such a rush of tributaries, the pool of available names expanded just as the Church's influence over what was acceptable diminished. The new saints were celebrities and stars of sport and stage and screen. Hollywood put names up in lights and a bratpack of Ritas, Garys and Deans joined the queue of Broadway babies as fans paid lip service at the font. Glamour was the game and Hollywood hopefuls who thought nothing of having a face-lift thought less of having a namedrop. They dreamed up names to suit their images: Norma Jean Baker became Marilyn Monroe and Dietrich, the former Maria Magdalena von Losch, condensed her names to coin the now-common 'Marlene'. Later, the rise of television, pulp fiction and romance magazines contributed a candyfloss of novelettish names while the muzibiz coined natureish names like Sky and Sun and Moon. But by the 1980s, Sloanedom, New Fogeydom, and Yuppiedom had retreated from the anarchy into tried and tested hand-me-downs: conservatism and conservation replaced chuckaway consumerism. Tradition was back with a bang.

That mood prevails still. Enter the right-on non-sexist, non-racist nineties in which quality is valued over the vagaries of fashion.

SOME NAME-DROPPERS

To	From
Julie Andrews	Julia Vernon
Lauren Bacall	Betty Joan Perski
Maria Callas	Maria Anna Sophia Cecilia Kalogeropoulos
Joan Crawford	Lucille Le Sueur
Judy Garland	Frances Gumm
Eric Clapton	Eric Clap
Tony Curtis	Bernard Schwartz
Rex Harrison	Reginald Cary
Boris Karloff	William Pratt
Leon Trotsky	Lev Davydovich Bronstein

SWOT-SPOT

- 'Joan Crawford' was the winning entry in a contest sponsored by her studio to find a new name for Lucille Le Sueur.
- François Marie Arouet used about 50 pen-names before settling on one. What was it? Voltaire.

Pitfalls and Problems
Ten traps to avoid

CHOOSING A NAME

As you begin the serious business of picking a name for your so-far un-named newcomer it's as well to consider a few general principles – even if you decide to throw them out with the baby's first bathwater.

Tricky Tonguetwisters

There's never been a bigger anthology of foreign tongue-twisters to give little Euro-Brits. But watch it: having a name that's hard to pronounce can spell problems for baby Tomaso. He says Tom-ahso and everyone else says Tom-ayso – on the telephone, over the tannoy, and even to his face. Never under-estimate the athleticism of the British when it comes to mis-pronounciation.

Looking for Trouble

Think aloud. Think twice. Think dirty. Always sound out possible first names in tandem with the surname, not in isolation, however splendid. Schoolmates will make mincemeat of Nora Bone and Mark Spencer, so try to spot any snigger factor before the baptism. The same is true of nicknames and abbreviations; you don't need a crystal ball to foresee the fate of Richard Head. And will Aurelia spend the unhappiest days of her life as 'Eel', Adrian as 'Aids', Dominic as 'Knickers'? You can't be completely governed by playground smut, but keep your innuendo up just high enough to see the really obvious googlies coming!

Awful Acronyms

When you've chosen first and middle names, have a quick contraction to ensure that no horrible acronym will result from your child's initials. It may not be the end of the world but, if it can be avoided, who wants MAD FAT HAG HIT DUD GAY PIG ASS

OVA TIT, BAD OLD COW! stamped into their luggage like a SUN headline? NIP IN BUD IF POSS.

Is it a Girl or a Boy?

It's quite common nowadays for parents to bestow unisex rather than gender-specific names in the belief that children so christened will avoid being cast in the traditional sex roles. There may be some truth in the theory, but parents considering androgynous options should think carefully about what is best for their child. Will s/he be teased at school? What will it be like going through life forever answering impertinent telephone enquiries as to which particular flavour of Sam, Chris, Pat or Jo you happen to be? At best it's a bore; at worst, gender insecurity may produce psychological pain. So do think it through – your Little Boy Blue may not be tickled pink when he clicks that he is the proverbial Boy Named Sue . . .

In Loving Memory?

It can be tempting to name a baby after a well-loved friend or relative. But don't get carried away. What suited your sainted aunt or grand old great-gran may stifle a nineties infant in mothballs and bombazine. Remember that you are giving a new life its own unique identity so don't just go with the Flo. Make sure you choose a name for its own sake, because you like it and because you think your child will like it, not simply as a memorial tribute to someone from another age.

Standing out from the Crowd

There is safety in numbers and the child with a very popular name may happily share it with many others, feeling comfortable and sheltered from teasing; alternatively, he or she may feel dull and unoriginal, one of a crowd with no distinguishing marks. But a child bearing a singular name will stand out and may be bullied by the peer group in the zoo of tiny fists. You can't poke a periscope into your baby's future, but you can hedge your bets by balancing a glamorous and sophisticated first name with a less extravagant second name or vice versa, giving children some flexibility of choice once they know their own minds.

Going OTT

Official forms tend to have space for three names – a first, a middle, and a surname. This has come about through custom and not because there is any rule governing the number of names to be carried by an individual. You can give your baby as many or as few as you like. But before you name the nappied one after a whole football team, remember all those forms he'll have to fill in.

Hollow Laughs

Under no circumstances can it be sensible to give your child a 'humorous' name. It may sound creasingly funny in the pub, but don't make your child live with what you consider to be wit. If it's a joke to you, then don't be surprised when your poor kid becomes a joke to everyone else. No butts, please, just don't do it. Why should the puns of the father be visited on the son? If you want a stupid name in your family, change your own. Then you can have a howling good laugh at your own expense. And so can the rest of us.

Dramatic Flops

If your child has one of the more frequently used surnames, while you'll probably want to zap it up with dramatic first and middle names, don't go berserk: Hannibal Smith and Indiana Jones may get away with murder, but will your teeny-weeny Smithereeny? By all means do the hotel industry a favour and deny the world another John Smith but keep a grip on reality. Don't try to hide your bushel under a light; whatever first name you tack on the front, Jones will remain plain honest Jones. Yet with a bit of thought, you'll come up with a first name that can distinguish without being outlandish.

'Have You Met Adolf?'

Every name carries with it the reflected glory of associations; it may conjure up a film star, or the rude, bald man next door, or a fictional character, or a mind-painting of some famous histori-cal personage. You should ponder any such associations because they are likely to affect other people's expectations of your child and, in turn, to burnish or tarnish your child's developing view of itself. Doesn't Raquel call up the busty beauty, Ebenezer the sour old miser, Adolf the Nazi dictator? In a world acutely conscious of image, be sure that any association-name you choose is not so hard to live up to – or to live down – that your child feels awkward under the burden of it.

Suffer the Little Children

Baptism

Nominal Christians

Britain is no longer a nation of God-lovers. But it is nevertheless a Christian country, especially when it's facing the facts
of life. Even committed atheists and uncommitted Dunnos
crave some token totemism when it comes to the crunch. We
may not practise what clergymen preach, yet we still like our
babies to start on the side of the angels, in the bosom of the
Church.

A Baptism of Faith

The word 'baptism' derives from the Greek, meaning 'to dip';
'christening' refers to the title Christ – 'christos' – given to Jesus
as Messiah. It means 'the Anointed'. Jesus asked John to
baptise Him in the River Jordan – hence water, representing
purification and rebirth, remains the central baptismal symbol
and it is sprinkled over each child upon its reception into the
Christian churches.

The Church of England admits babies by the rite usually
known as christening. The names given during the ceremony
are called Christian names and these are agreed between the
minister and the parents; the Church does not impose its
authority in the process. During the service, the godparents
publicly accept responsibility for the child's upbringing in the
Anglican faith.

Babies are received into the Roman Catholic Church by the
ceremony known as baptism. The Church traditionally requires
that at least one of the names bestowed is that of a saint; the
saint is then held to become the baby's patron, taking a kindly
and protective interest in its life. The godparents, who must
themselves be baptised members of the Catholic faith, become
the baby's spiritual guardians and they are given the lighted
candle that represents the little soul, now shining with the light
of Christ.

Tot Bits:

- The white robe or shawl put on the newly anointed baby is called the 'chrisom-cloth'.

- Scholars think that John the Baptist copied his immersion course from a strict Dead Sea sect called the Essenes. A form of baptism was one of their chief rites.

- If safe delivery was unlikely, a midwife used to christen the baby before birth with ambisexual names such as Vitalis, Creature, and Chylde-of-God. St Augustine said Hell was paved with unbaptised babies, but the Church no longer holds that view.

- Baptists believe only total over-the-top dunking is proper baptism.

- It took the minister over *two* minutes to read the litany of 140 names given to young Tracey . . . Etc . . . Wilson at her christening in 1991.

- The US president Harry S. Truman was christened just that. The 'S' doesn't stand for anything.

- John the Baptist is the patron saint of tailors.

Naming Names

From registration to deed poll

Registering the Birth

In accordance with the Registration Act, which came into force on 1 July 1837, every baby born in England or Wales must be registered within 42 days of its birth. It's the law's way of saying 'Welcome to the human race'.

The baby must be registered where it was born. Every large town has a Register Office and it's here that the date and place of birth, the baby's sex, surname and the given names are all recorded.

Don't worry if you haven't chosen the names; the law does not rush you in this important decision. If the baby's names are not available in the first six weeks, the mother's maiden name and the father's occupation are recorded instead. There is also room to add the mother's occupation.

In fact, although the baby must be 'booked' at birth, names can be added at the bottom of the birth certificate for another twelve months.

If the baby's parents are not married, a rather regrettable and old-fashioned system applies. The father's details will be recorded only if he accompanies the mother to the Register Office or if he provides written recognition of the child as his own.

Changing a Name

If your baby later wants to switch any or all of its names, there is no problem. Although the original birth record cannot be revised, fresh documents can be lodged. In fact, even these are not necessary; so long as you inform the taxman about changes in your current identity, you are free to call yourself anything you please – provided that it is *not* for fraudulent purposes, or in breach of the copyright and obscenity laws.

Anyone serious about Robin' Peter to be Paul is, however, likely to want a documentary record – with lots of official-looking sealing wax, the blobbier the better. Failing that, a rubber stamp.

The first and cheapest way of changing your name in a way which provides written proof is the swearing of a Statutory Declaration before a Commissioner for Oaths, usually at a solicitor's office. This method is legal, official, and for a few quid gives you a piece of paper to flourish. For most people, this should answer their purpose.

There is, however, an even loftier, more legal, even *more* official method of eating your parents' words. Called the Deed Poll, it's generally used by people who need maximum authentication for a change of identity; someone who is to be chartered in a profession, for example, or planning to enter a complicated business partnership. The deed is sworn, stamped, then enrolled at the Supreme Court at a cost of fifty pounds and a penny.

But do remember that none of these methods allows you to disappear. That would turn the birth certificate into a *carte blanche* for criminals. Your original record at St Catherine's House is not tampered with; subsequent alterations are merely addenda.

> For more information you can contact:
> The Office of Population & Censuses
> St Catherine's House
> 10 Kingsway
> London WC2B 6JP

Stylefile
Coming or Going?

Fashionability

One man's style becomes another man's fashion. Isn't fashion just personal style gone public and enjoying a brief blaze of glory? But if a fashion outlives its uselessness then it may achieve dignity as a classic of lasting consequence. Everyone has style. We show it in where we live, in what we wear, in how we display. Style, unlike taste, cannot be acquired, and some people wear life so stylishly that their style is Style; it looks at the present and sees the future. You've either got it or you'll never get it.

If you opt for the fashionable or the classic in naming your baby, the choice will reflect your cultural awareness; if you reject both in favour of the original, you'll reflect your own style by breaking moulds, setting trends, making fashion.

Here to Stay?

Picking a name to outlast the century is an adventure. You can be an explorer blazing your own trail, or you can be a tourist, following the beaten track. Either way, you'll probably get bogged down. You want something accessible yet not too available; you want something idiosyncratic yet not too eccentric; you want something with a past which still has a future. So how *do* you pick?

Well, you could start by eliminating the recently trendy names whose popularity has peaked and lost its gloss through overexposure. They've **Come and Gone**. More positively, you can join the dig for anything old-fangled; why not pick names from your ancestral tombstones? They've been so long dead and buried that they're now **Up and Coming**. And most daringly, you can embrace the real old **Down and Outs** whom nobody's loved for ages. Among all the has-beens and never-weres, you might just find a dazzling will-be.

Come and Gone

The following tots topped the pops in 1991–92. Victims of their own success, these delightful names should now come with riot shields. Hannah and her sisters will crowd into school just before your child. Be warned if you go for one of these classy little charmers: they could be here today and everywhere tomorrow.

POPULAR GIRLS

Alice	Emma	Olivia
Amanda	Georgina	Rachel
Amy	Hannah	Rebecca
Catherine	Jessica	Samantha
Charlotte	Lauren	Sarah
Chloe	Lisa	Sophie
Emily		

POPULAR BOYS

Adam	Edward	Josh
Alex	Henry	Michael
Alexander	Jack	Oliver
Ben	Jake	Samuel
Charles	James	Thomas
Christopher	Jamie	William
Daniel	Jason	

- 1991's top-name list in *The Times*, collated from
  announcements in its own Births column, placed the
  winning names in the following order of popularity:
  GIRLS – Emily, Charlotte, Olivia, Sophie, Lucy, Emma,
  Sarah, Georgina, Alice, Hannah; BOYS – James,
  Alexander, Thomas, William, Edward, Charles, Oliver,
  George, Henry, Samuel. But an alternative list produced
  by the *Mail on Sunday*, using nationwide birth records for
  the year, ranked the names thus: GIRLS – Rebecca,
  Sarah, Jessica, Hannah, Lauren, Emma, Sophie,
  Samantha, Chloe, Catherine; BOYS – Daniel, Thomas,
  Samuel, James, Christopher, Jamie, Adam, Michael,
  Alexander, Jack.

On the whole, good old-fashioned names are the now thing.
Making way for them is the whole dynasty of furry-dice fads
acquired from soaps, pop stars, and fanzines. We're pro-
Europe now, and Americanisms have had their day. We're eco-
friendly and Seventies glitter doesn't biodegrade. Carin'n'sharin
is IN and Karen'n'Sharon are OUT, sunk – with every Trace –
somewhere in the stereotypes of television sitcom. A few may
survive, but the following bimbosities and rambosities, which
dominated the popularity stakes for a decade, have finally
Come and Gone.

FEMALES FALLEN FROM FAVOUR

Barbra	**Cher**	**Darlene**
Bianca	**Cheryl**	**Dawn**
Bonnie	**Cherry**	**Dayle**
Carly	**Dana**	**Debbi**
Charlene	**Danni**	**Donna**

Fallon	Maxi	Sharon
Karen	Melody	Sheena
Kelly	Roxy	Sherry
Kim	Sabrina	Stacey
Krystle	Sade	Tammy
Kylie	Sadie	Tiffany
Lorraine	Sandi	Tracey
Lulu	Sasha	Trixie
Marlene		

SWOT-SPOT

- Kylie means 'boomerang' in Western Australia – so expect this name to come back!

LOUTS WHO ARE OUT

Barry	Gavin	Ross
Blake	Glenn	Ryan
Burt	Kelvin	Scott
Carl	Kevin	Shane
Craig	Kim	Stewart
Curt	Kirk	Todd
Darren	Lance	Troy
Darryl	Marvin	Vic
Denzil	Melvin	Vince
Derek	Rex	Warren
Dirk	Rick	Wayne
Gary		

Tired and Tested

Also badly in need of a rest are many once-swinging names, very popular from the Sixties to the Eighties and now grey with mettle fatigue. They say flares, not flair.

FADING FAST

Anita	Janice	Nancy
Annabel	Jayne	Nanette
Beverley	Jean	Nicole
Carol	Joanne	Noreen
Christine	Joyce	Norma
Cleo	Judy	Paula
Colleen	Kay	Pauline
Dale	Kimberley	Raquel
Danielle	Kirsty	Renee
Deborah	Linda	Rita
Denise	Lindsay	Sandra
Diane	Lisa	Sheila
Dinah	Lois	Shelley
Eileen	Loretta	Shirley
Gail	Marilyn	Tara
Glenda	Maxine	Tina
Gloria	Megan	Trudy
Glynis	Melanie	Vanessa
Jade	Melissa	Wendy
Jan	Moira	Yasmin
Janet	Monica	

OVER AND OUT

Adrian	Garth	Nigel
Alan	Glyn	Paul
Alec	Gordon	Raymond
Bernard	Graham	Rodney
Brent	Grant	Ronald
Brian	Howard	Rory
Brody	Jeffrey	Roy
Bruce	Keith	Russell
Bryan	Kenneth	Shaw
Colin	Larry	Steven
Dean	Lee	Stuart
Dennis	Leonard	Terry
Desmond	Malcolm	Tony
Don	Martin	Trevor
Donald	Mervyn	Victor
Dudley	Neil	Vincent
Eamon		

Up and Coming Names

Trad is hot and fad is not. Britain is taking out the trash, and with it, Trixie, Dixie, Tel, Del et Al. Now we're eager to break old ground – and the newest names for the hottest tots are those with rustic and religious roots, the squarer the better.

Names generally take at least a century to rise, fall and re-emerge – hence, some of the most approachable **Up and**

Comings were all the rage with our grandparents and their housemaids. Neglected throughout the Sixties and Seventies, these old-fashioned names began coming back during the conservative revival of the Eighties. Some have already zoomed into the **Come and Gone** category, but don't let that worry you!

GOLDEN OLDIE GIRLS

Anna	Kitty (Katherine)
Annie	Lillian
Beatrice	Lily
Bess	Mabel
Cissie (Cecilia)	Maisie (Margaret)
Clara	Maud
Connie (Constance)	Meg (Margaret)
Daisy (Margaret)	Millie (Millicent)
Ellen	Molly (Margaret)
Elsie (Elizabeth/Elspeth)	Nellie (Helen)
Faith	Peggy (Margaret)
Fanny (Frances)	Polly
Grace	Queenie (Regina)
Gussie (Augusta)	Sally
Hannah	Tabitha
Harriet	Tilly (Matilda)
Hetty (Henrietta/Heather)	Winnie (Winifred)
Hope	

GOLDEN OLDIE GUYS

Abe	**Jed** (Jedediah)
Barnaby	**Jethro**
Barney	**Jock** (John)
Bart (Bartholomew)	**Joe** (Joseph)
Benet (Benedict)	**Josh** (Joshua)
Bram	**Joss** (Josiah)
Brewster	**Judd**
Cal (Callum/Calvin)	**Kester** (Christopher)
Caleb	**Kit** (Christopher)
Chad	**Luke**
Clay	**Max** (Maxwell/Maximillian)
Clem (Clement)	**Nat** (Nathan/Nathaniel)
Dickon (Richard)	**Ned** (Edward/Edmund)
Digby	**Seth**
Diggory	**Silas**
Frank	**Simm** (Simon)
Fred	**Tam**
Gabriel	**Zack**
Gus (Augustine)	**Zak** (Zachary/Isaac)
Jake (Jacob)	

Evergreen Names

There is a vicar's tea party of names which keep on going and are never gone. From Agincourt to Armageddon, they're never

Out, never In, ever green. Beyond fashion, **Evergreens** are not part of the great revival, since they've never been away. Evergreens are part of the English heritage; standing firm under the oaks, they saw off the Armada, Napoleon, Fritz, and the Jerries – just as they've seen off the Thoms, the Diks and the Haris.

EVERGREEN GIRLS

Alice	Eleanor	Kate
Anne	Elizabeth	Katharine
Catherine	Emma	Margaret
Cecily	Jane	Mary
Clare	Joan	

EVERGREEN BOYS

Christopher	James	Robin
Edward	John	Roger
Geoffrey	Michael	Stephen
Henry	Nicholas	Thomas
Hugh	Richard	Walter
Jack	Robert	William

SWOT-SPOT

- Fourteenth-century records show that 64 per cent of the male English population was called Henry, John, Richard, Robert or William.
- Mediaeval nicknames had rhyming forms, like Rick, Dick, and Hick for Richard, Hodge for Roger, and Hob and Bob for Robert. Their use was so general that 'hodge' became a common noun, meaning country labourer, 'hick' came to mean a backward yokel, and 'jack' and 'dick' described any ordinary fellow.

Classy Classics

Some names always hold their charm, whatever the fashion. They're never at the top of the polls but they never fall from grace either, and they'll never date your child. They may lack the unbroken tradition of the **Evergreens** – but then, they spring from a more varied landscape than the trampled English lawn.

CLASSY GIRLS

Alexandra	Frances	Madeline
Alison	Francesca	Nicola
Amanda	Gemma	Ruth
Belinda	Gillian	Sarah
Caroline	Julia	Stephanie
Charlotte	Laura	Susan
Diana	Louise	Susannah
Fiona	Lucy	Victoria

CLASSY BOYS

Alexander	Giles	Mark
Andrew	Guy	Matthew
Antony	Hamish	Patrick
Benjamin	Ian	Peter
Charles	Jeremy	Philip
Daniel	Jonathan	Seamus
David	Julian	Sebastian
George	Justin	Simon
Gerald	Luke	

New Names for Old

Even if you've set your heart on a name among either the **Come and Gones** or the common but **Classy Classics**, there's room for manoeuvre if you wish. It's easy to make subtle substitutions whilst still keeping to the spirit of your original choice. Now we're all Europeans, why not show fresh Nineties savvy by using foreign or historic counterparts for British bores? Remember, Giuseppe Verdi is just Joe Green! And with the current fashion for weird and wonderful old names, you can plunder the Romans, the Greeks and the Celts for their rusting treasure.

NEW GIRLS FOR OLD

Alicia	Finola	Louisa
Aliza	Flavia	Lucienne
Alyssum	Flora	Lucrece
Aurelia	Francine	Miranda
Aurora	Francisca	Odette
Cassandra	Franziske	Rhea
Charlotta	Georgiana	Rosana
Chloris	Giulietta	Rowena
Christiane	Hella	Rumer
Clarissa	Jocasta	Sabina
Domenica	Juliana	Samira
Eliza	Justina	Sophia
Elsa	Laurel	Tamara
Elysia	Livia	

NEW BOYS FOR OLD

Abe	Christian	Marcel
Aidan	Crispin	Marcus
Alban	Duncan	Mikhail
Aldous	Dunstan	Olivier
Aubrey	Edmund	Oscar
Augustine (Gus)	Fergus	Owen
Bede	Fingal	Rafe
Bram	Finn	Ralph
Brock	Gervase	Rupert
Bruno	Jerome	Toby
Callum	Julius	Tristram
Carlos		

Blasts from the Past

If you're confident of your own style and have the guts to prove it, you can make your baby one in a million by choosing a name that isn't fashionable, never will be, and never was. Call up the shining rabble of forgotten emperors, goddesses, saints, princes, heroes, or the romantic lovers of legend, and steal a one-off cast-off that's less a talking point than a conversation piece. Among the old bones passed over by mainstream fashion, there are buried treasures to replace the hackneyed and obvious. It's surprising how lost-and-foundlings can scrub up into something really special. If you like the name Edward, say, but not in the plural, try Edric instead. It's just as user-friendly, teddy-wise. It's just as royal, more ancient, and utterly singular.

PASSED MISTRESSES

Adeline	Charis	Ernestine
Albertine	Christabel	Erwina
Albina	Chryseis	Estelle
Albreda	Clarice	Estrild
Alda	Clarinda	Eugenia
Alfreda	Clementine	Eulalia
Ambrosine	Coralie	Eunice
Amice	Corisande	Eveline
Ariadne	Cornelia	Faustine
Asphodel	Crispina	Felicia
Aurea	Damaris	Flavia
Basilia	Delilah	Fredegonde
Beatrix	Dido	Freya
Berengaria	Dilys	Fronde
Berengiere	Dionysia	Frusannah
Blasia	Druella	Fulvia
Bonita	Drusilla	Galiena
Britannia	Eda	Ghislaine
Brunella	Eglentyne	Gilda
Brynhild	Electra	Ginevra
Calandra	Elfreda	Glenda
Calypso	Ellice	Godiva
Candace	Eloise	Gracilia
Candia	Elysia	Grania
Celosia	Emmeline	Guinevere
Cerelia	Enid	Gwendolyn

PASSED MISTRESSES

Haidee	Lyris	Olinda
Halcyone	Mab	Oralia
Hebe	Madora	Ordelia
Honoria	Malvina	Oriana
Horatia	Mara	Oriel
Hortensia	Marcella	Pallas
Huette	Marelda	Panthea
Ignatia	Mavis	Pernella
Ileana	Medea	Persephone
Isadora	Melantha	Persis
Isis	Melina	Petrina
Ismay	Melinda	Petronella
Isolda	Melora	Phaedra
Jacinda	Mercia	Philana
Jacobina	Meriel	Placida
Jarvia	Messina	Pomona
Jovita	Mimosa	Prospera
Justina	Morgana	Prunella
Lavinia	Morwenna	Pyrena
Leda	Musette	Radella
Letitia	Nadia	Rae
Lettice	Nairne	Raina
Linnet	Nara	Rhea
Loveday	Nellwyn	Ricarda
Lucasta	Nissa	Richenda
Lucilla	Odelia	Rilla

PASSED MISTRESSES

Roanna	Salena	Sophronia
Robina	Savina	Sorrel
Romaine	Saxona	Thera
Romola	Sebastiane	Tizane
Rosabel	Semele	Valentina
Rosetta	Seraphina	Verena
Rufina	Serilda	Vespera
Rula	Sidra	Vita
Saba	Sirena	Zuleika

PASSED MASTERS

Abelard	Argos	Cadmus
Aelfric	Ariel	Cadoc
Aeneas	Athelstan	Caradoc
Aiken	Auberon	Chad
Ajax	Baldric	Clement
Alard	Baldwin	Clovis
Alaric	Baptist	Cormac
Alberic	Bardolf	Cuthbert
Aldous	Barnard	Cynric
Aldred	Barnet	Cyprian
Aldwin	Bayard	Cyrus
Algar	Bevis	Damon
Alwyn	Blase	Darius
Amory	Brewster	Dorian
Archard	Brutus	Drogo

PASSED MASTERS

Dunstan	Gamal	Jevon
Edgar	Garret	Jivin
Edred	Garridan	Jolyon
Edric	Gaston	Joubert
Edwold	Gawain	Jovett
Egmont	Geraint	Julius
Egon	Giffard	Kay
Eldon	Godric	Kendrick
Eldwin	Godwin	Kentigern
Embert	Gordion	Lambert
Emerick	Griffin	Lancelot
Esmund	Griffith	Leander
Everard	Griswald	Leofric
Fabian	Hadrian	Leofwin
Fabius	Hakon	Linus
Farquhar	Hector	Lionel
Festus	Hereward	Lucas
Fingal	Hobart	Lucius
Finn	Horatio	Lytton
Florian	Ignatius	Madoc
Frey	Ingram	Magnus
Fulke	Inigo	Marius
Fursey	Isidore	Marmaduke
Gabriel	Ivar	Mauger
Galahad	Jarvis	Maynard
Galen	Jethro	Medric

PASSED MASTERS

Merlin	Pepin	Saxon
Merryn	Peregrine	Senan
Mortimer	Perkin	Serle
Ninian	Perran	Silas
Noel	Petroc	Siward
Odin	Phileas	Swithin
Odo	Phineas	Talbot
Offa	Piers	Tancred
Orestes	Priam	Teige
Orion	Quintin	Thorkell
Orson	Rafe	Thurstan
Osbert	Ranulf	Titus
Osmund	Raoul	Torquil
Osric	Raven	Tybalt
Oswald	Remus	Valerian
Oswin	Reynard	Vitas
Ovid	Rollo	Wulfram
Pagan	Ronan	Wulfric
Pancras	Rowan	Wulfstan
Paris	Ruffin	Wystan
Patrin	Sacheverell	

Mouldy Oldies

Whilst everyone agrees there's a strong trend towards good old-fashioned names, there *are* one or two fuddy-duddies which really should stay in the closet with the doors firmly locked. They're the Frumps. They wear pinnies and curlers and they drink port and lemon. Then there are the Grumps. They wear cycling clips and talk about nothing but their enormous marrows and what they did in the Blitz. Although Frumpy Grumpy names are by no means classless, they are sexless and colourless.

FRUMPY

Agatha	Flo	Maud
Dorcas	Gertrude	Mildred
Doreen	Gladys	Morag
Doris	Hilda	Muriel
Edith	Irene	Myra
Edna	Irma	Olive
Enid	Mabel	Oona
Ethel		

GRUMPY

Archibald	Eric	Norman
Arnold	Ernest	Percy
Arthur	Godfrey	Reginald
Ebenezer	Harold	Rodney
Egbert	Humphrey	Stanley

Little Gems

The Victorian fancy for prettifying and petrifying girls into gems was a whimsical conceit which left no stone unturned, though it never spread to boys. But the following dazzling names will be back in the Neolithic Nineties. And perhaps this time they'll bring a landslide of Granites, Slates, Flints and Grits to join those old cavemen Chip, Rock and Cliff?

DAZZLING DAMSELS

Amber	Emerald	Opal
Amethyst	Esmeralda	Pearl
Beryl	Garnet	Petra
Coral	Goldie	Ruby
Crystal	Iona	Sapphira
Diamanta	Jacinth	Sapphire
Diamond	Jade	Topaz
Emblem	Jewel	

Flower Girls

The Victorians loved pressing flowers, even on to their baby girls. As the Industrial Revolution flourished, floral names achieved popularity for their innocence and freshness in an age of growing complexity. Now we, too, are falling for flower power. Some of these names had a long life below stairs; others began swirling into the salons on the heels of herbaceous bawds like Lillie Langtry and Violet Keppel, gaining a modern respectability with Princess Margaret Rose. A few sprigs – like Yasmin, Laura and Jasmine – have already **Come and Gone**, but the following are ripe for the plucking.

FLOWER GIRLS

Anemone	Heather	Orchid
Anthea	Holly	Pansy
Azalea	Hyacinth	Poppy
Blossom	Iris	Posy
Bryony	Ivy	Primrose
Camelia	Jessamine	Rose
Celandine	Jonquil	Rosemary
Clover	Juniper	Sage
Dahlia	Laurel	Salvia
Daisy	Lavender	Verbena
Eglantyne	Lilac	Viola
Fern	Lily	Violet
Fleur	Magnolia	Violetta
Flora	Marigold	Willow
Gardenia	Mimosa	Zinnia
Hazel	Myrtle	

Heavenly Babes

The current impulse towards everything honest and genuine is likely to revive the Virtue abstracts. Sober but elegant, expect a fresh batch of names high in moral fibre – full of goodness, not much fun!

GOOD GIRLS

Charity	Grace	Modesty
Comfort	Honoria	Patience
Constance	Honour	Prudence
Faith	Hope	Verity
Felicity	Joy	

I want it now!

P A T I E N C E

Derring-doers

Whilst boys are excluded from the stone, flower and virtue revivals, they're in like Flynn for the comeback of derring-do. These laughing cavaliers breeze in with a dashing insouciance from the days when chaps were chaps – on horses, in biplanes, or in boaters. No gravity, all levity, Boy's Own and Boyhood-of-Raleigh, they are far too fickle and charming for anyone's good, even their own.

FLASHMEN

Alistair	Felix	Miles
Angus	Gerard	Neville
Basil	Hilary	Roland
Bertram	Hugo	Rufus
Clive	Jasper	Tristan
Damian	Jocelyn	Valentine
Dougal	Lucian	Vivian
Douglas		

Little Gipsies: *Born to be Wild . . .*

When Moonlighter Bruce Willis named his little pixie Rumer Glenn, he was taking a walk on the wild side. Gipsy-names are again rumbling up the green lanes as part of the revival of interest in anything fresh and ecologically sound. And nothing is fresher than the rain-washed names of Romany romance. Close to the earth, they bubble straight from the heart, speaking of kinship and nature.

GIPSY ROSES

Choomia – kiss   **Rawnie** – lady
Dudee – star   **Rumer** – gipsy
Miri – my own   **Tasarla** – dawn and dusk

GIPSY KINGS

Bal – fine head of hair
Bavol – air
Bersh – one-year
Besh – one-year
Bor – hedge
Bowle – snail
Brishan – born in the rain
Camlo – lovely
Cappi – good luck
Chik – earth
Dukker – bewitcher
Durriken – bewitcher
Durril – berry
Fordel – forgive
Garridan – you hid
Gillie – song
Jibben – life
Jivvil – life
Kerey – homeward-bound
Kistur – rider
Lel – he takes
Lendar – from his parents
Lennor – spring and summer

Lensar – with his parents
Lutherum – slumber
Mander – from myself
Merripen – life and death
Nav – name
Nev – name
Pal – brother
Patrin – trailblazer
Pattin – leaf
Pias – fun
Pov – earth
Simen – likeness
Stiggur – gateway
Tas – bird's nest
Tawno – tiny
Tobbar – life's open road
Wen – winter
Wesh – wood
Yarb – sweet herb

Norse Names: *Blowing a Gael!*

Doing the Highland Fling, the Irish jig or sounding Nordic or Celtic is **HOT** – but mostly for chilly Anglo-Saxons, who are going berserk for anything Norse or Celtic. They'll take anything Ossianic or Pictish, anything nice and Norsey where Gaels skirl over rock and ice.

VALKYRIES

Andra	Ena	Meraud
Angharad	Freya	Morna
Bevin	Guinevere	Morwenna
Blodwen	Gwawr	Myfanwy
Bronwen	Idris	Nara
Bryna	Ilka	Nora
Ceridwen	Inge	Ola
Cymry	Iona	Olwyn
Dagmar	Kara	Ran
Dilys	Maeve	Tangye
Douana	Mairead	Tanith
Eiluned	Mairin	Tegan
Eithne	Maura	Valda

But beware the following Valkyries. They've **Come and Gone.** To Valhalla.

Brenda	Megan	Sheena
Bridget	Moira	Shona
Deirdre	Nuala	Sinead
Glynis	Rhonda	Thora
Gwyneth	Selma	Wanda
Keely		

VIKINGS

Aegir	Dugald	Ingram
Aneurin	Erskine	Ivar
Angus	Farrel	Kane
Asgard	Farquhar	Kanute
Balder	Fergal	Leif
Beck	Fergus	Liam
Brage	Fingal	Loki
Brand	Finn	Mabry
Cadoc	Flyn	Mac
Cadwallader	Frey	Madoc
Cai	Fursey	Merryn
Callum	Gabbo	Mordred
Caradoc	Gael	Odin
Chiel	Galahad	Olaf
Ciaran	Garth	Olav
Colwyn	Gawain	Owen
Conal	Geraint	Rafferty
Conan	Gowan	Roarke
Conor	Griffith	Seamus
Dai	Guntar	Sigurd
Delaney	Haakon	Tavish
Dermot	Hamish	Teague
Diarmuid	Helgi	Thor
Dougal	Herne	

Continental Names: *We're All in Europe Now*

Europe's **IN** for Britain, including the area that was Curtained off. In the common European home, we are rediscovering our common linguistic root from which Slavonic, Greek, Germanic, Celtic and even Sanskrit derive. While the Natashas and Marias have already **Come and Gone**, European names offer plenty of other **Up and Coming** choices.

RUSSIA		POLAND	
Girls	Boys	Girls	Boys
Anastasia	Alexandr	Alina	Andrej
Antonina	Alexi	Aniela	Anzelm
Evelina	Andrei	Celina	Borys
Galina	Boris	Felcia	Casimir
Irina	Daveed	Franciscka	Franek
Katya	Dmitri	Janina	Janos
Kira	Feodor	Joanna	Jarek
Larissa	Grigori	Karolina	Karol
Ludmilla	Igor	Kassia	Lech
Natalya	Ivan	Lillianna	Lukasz
Olga	Konstantine	Marinna	Marian
Sofia	Mikhail	Marta	Mateusz
Tatiana	Nikolai	Raisa	Tomasz
Yelena	Oleg	Stasha	Zarek
	Roman	Zofia	
	Stefan		
	Vladimir		
	Yuri		

HUNGARY		SCANDINAVIA	
Girls	Boys	Girls	Boys
Anezka	Dorjan	Anneka	Anders
Danica	Erno	Astrid	Audun
Fania	Jeno	Berta	Bjorn
Ilona	Karoly	Britta	Dag
Katerina	Karsten	Dagmar	Erik
Lilike	Kito	Erma	Finn
Marika	Odon	Eva	Gunnar
Tereza	Piotr	Grete	Gustaf
Tesia	Vilmos	Hanne	Hans
		Hilde	Ingvar
		Ingrid	Jens
		Kari	Karl
		Karin	Kristian
		Liv	Lars
		Margareda	Morten
		Marit	Nils
		Signe	Olaf
		Toril	Oskar
		Ulla	Per
		Ulrika	Rolf

GERMANY		FRANCE	
Girls	Boys	Girls	Boys
Amalie	Arno	Anais	Alain
Annalise	Ernst	Ariane	Andre
Brigitta	Gunter	Camille	Bruno
Elfie	Hans	Cecile	Clement
Elke	Johann	Eugenie	Didier
Gretchen	Karl	Francoise	Edouard
Heidi	Kaspar	Jeanette	Etienne
Katja	Klaus	Laure	Jacques
Mina	Konrad	Lucienne	Julienne
Monika	Leopold	Mariette	Luc
Petra	Ludwig	Marine	Raul
Senta	Wilhelm	Silvie	Thierry

SPAIN		ITALY	
Girls	Boys	Girls	Boys
Ana	Alejandro	Adriana	Adriano
Blanca	Carlos	Allegra	Alessandro
Carmela	Enrique	Carlotta	Antonio
Consuela	Enzo	Chiara	Carmelo
Elena	Federico	Gabriella	Eugenio
Estrella	Francisco	Giovanna	Francesco
Luisa	Luis	Isabella	Giorgio
Margarida	Manuel	Lia	Gregorio
Marisol	Orlando	Lucia	Lorenzo

SPAIN

Girls	Boys
Pilar	Pedro
Sarita	Rafael
Serafina	Raul
Sofia	

ITALY

Girls	Boys
Oriana	Rosario
Renata	Saberio
Rosina	Salvatore
Silvana	Taddeo
Vittoria	Vittorio

GREECE

Girls	Boys
Aphrodite	Aristotle
Athena	Christos
Chrisoula	Claudios
Clio	Constantine
Cosima	Cosmo
Elektra	Dimitri
Eleni	Kyriako
Kalliope	Nikolos
Katina	Panayiotis
Olympia	Petros
Pallas	Stavros
Stephania	Theodor
	Yeorgi

Names and Places

In the United States, there is a new desire to name children after places – Grace Slick called her daughter China, Don Johnson his son Dakota, and the President himself has a daughter called Chelsea. While it's still rare to find geographical babies in Britain, India Hicks – bridesmaid to the Princess of Wales – introduced a worldly note, and the year 1991–92 put Chelsea firmly on the map in Essex, where it came third in the charts. It seems likely that this trend will develop into high fashion as parents seek offbeat, individual names that are nevertheless tied to tradition. Beyond the obvious allure of euphony or mere snobbery, place names are neuter and may be chosen to honour ancient family roots, or to remember happy holidays. Putting a name to a place and the place to a face is absolutely personal, but the following are already in uncommon use.

CITY GIRLS

Alexandria	Florence	Paris
Asia	Geneva	Persia
Brittany	Georgia	Roma
Carolina	Holland	Siena
Catalina	India	Venetia
Chelsea	Kent	Venezia
China	Odessa	Venice
Devon		

Image
Selling Your Baby!

Engineering an Image

Names. They're encoded tittle-tattle, telling tales to strangers about a person not yet met. They drop hints of class, background, aspiration; they play upon the imagination and transmit potent gossip about what the person is like.

Names, like people, have personalities. They puff smoke signals into the unknown – intellectual, reliable, glamorous, pretty, tarty, capable, handsome, ugly, common, posh. You name it – they'll think it! Image-names carry baggage – usually someone else's. What does Marilyn say to you? Madonna? On paper, Rupert and Kelvin, Trixiebell and Augusta project sharply different images on which outsiders will base outrageous assumptions. Someone with a frivolous name may find it hard to be taken seriously.

But image is not just about how the world sees you. It's about how you see yourself. As your own name subtly changed you, the name you choose for your baby will make its mark. Some names are hard to live up to – a boy given a Rambo name may grow into a Rambo man. Or he may sob himself to sleep because he can't live up to the image. Be careful: liking a name is one thing, but living in it is another. Imagine the teacher shouting it at Assembly. Picture getting it on a CV. After trying it for sighs, if the name satisfies your ear and seems baby-apt, then you've done your best. A name is a gift; it says more about the parents' tastes and their hopes for the baby than it does about the infant in question.

Remember, stereotyping can work to your advantage and you can develop into the image that your name suggests. Positive Image Names basically fall into the brackets Brainy, Classy, Proactive and Arty. But if you're worried about burdening your bairn with expectations, there are plenty of Janets and Johns scattered throughout this book who come with no image and no baggage.

Brainy Names

Brainy names speak volumes. They tell the world that your baby comes from a cultivated home. Anyone from a similar background will read the signs and take an interest in your child. Brainy names are particularly useful for girls since they imply horn-rimmed brainpower, some degree – a Double First – of bookishness, and an A-level in Earnesty. Under the Flopsy Bunny duvet, you'll catch them reading philosophy by the light of an exhausted torch. Happiest with their noses in books and their feet in footnotes, these clever-clogs soon grow too big for their bootees.

BLUESTOCKINGS

Abigail	Clementine	Helen
Adele	Constance	Henrietta
Agatha	Deirdre	Hester
Agnes	Edith	Irene
Aileen	Edwina	Joan
Alice	Emily	Josephine
Andrea	Ernestine	Joyce
Anna	Esther	Judith
Audrey	Eugenia	Kate
Bertha	Eunice	Martha
Blanche	Frances	Matilda
Bronwen	Gertrude	Moira
Catherine	Glenda	Monica
Cecilia	Grace	Morag
Clarissa	Hannah	Nadia
Claudia	Harriet	Natalie

BLUESTOCKINGS

Nora	Priscilla	Ursula
Norma	Rachel	Vanessa
Paula	Rebecca	Virginia
Penelope	Ruth	Winifred

SWOT-SPOT

- Legend tells how Princess Ursula, a Christian Briton, wanted to stay a virgin so badly that she sailed away with 11,000 female chums to dodge wedlock. But the flotilla was blown up the Rhine where its nunly cargo was promptly murdered by the Huns. Why? Because hard-to-get Ursula didn't fancy the chief!

MASTERMINDS

Alec	Crispin	Gordon
Ambrose	Cyril	Graham
Basil	Daniel	Gregory
Benjamin	Dominic	Horace
Bernard	Edgar	Hubert
Calvin	Edwin	Humphrey
Cedric	Eric	Jacob
Christopher	Ernest	Jeremy
Clarence	Eugene	Jerome
Claude	Francis	Julian
Clement	Gabriel	Justin
Clovis	Gerald	Leonard
Conrad	Gilbert	Lionel
Cornelius	Godfrey	Luke

MASTERMINDS

Magnus	Philip	Tobias
Matthew	Quentin	Urban
Maurice	Simon	Walter
Mortimer	Solomon	Wilfrid
Norman	Theodore	Winston
Owen	Timothy	Wystan

SWOT-SPOT

- 'Namby-pamby', meaning feeble and wimpish, was a nickname given to the poet Ambrose Phillips (1674–1749) whose treacly odes to children were mocked by eighteenth-century Tories.

Upwardly Mobile Names

Family, school, college, and profession still define what we are and what our children will be. But nowadays the whole social system is more relaxed, mobile if not exactly fluid, and it's easier for people to break into the charmed circle by their own efforts. And we can name our children for that upwardly mobile future. Even if we don't have silver-spoons ourselves, we can give them to our youngsters. So why not give your heirs graces and the sheen of a thoroughbred? Your baby can sound as upper-crust and chinless as the best of them. But it means discarding Trashion: pop-star names are out, made-up names are out, soap-opera names are out, and names that too obviously pay court to money and power are out for any scion serious about acquiring pedigree poise.

UPPER CRUST GELS

Alexandra	Charlotte	Miranda
Amelia	Charmian	Olivia
Anastasia	Clarissa	Pandora
Antonia	Claudia	Patricia
Arabella	Cressida	Petronella
Araminta	Diana	Philomena
Beatrice	Eugenia	Phyllida
Beatrix	Francesca	Phyllis
Camilla	Frederica	Sophia
Candida	Henrietta	Tabitha
Carola	Imogen	Tamsin
Carolina	Jessica	Thomasina
Caroline	Lavinia	Vanessa
Cassandra	Letitia	Venetia
Charis	Lucinda	Victoria
Charlotta	Michaela	Virginia

UPPER CRUST CHAPS

Alexander	Christian	Eugene
Algernon	Clarence	Evelyn
Archibald	Cyril	Francis
Aubrey	Douglas	Frederick
Basil	Edgar	George
Cecil	Edmund	Gerard
Charles	Edward	Gilbert

UPPER CRUST CHAPS

Giles	Leopold	Ranulf
Granville	Lionel	Roderick
Guy	Marmaduke	Roland
Hector	Maximilian	Rowland
Henry	Ninian	Rupert
Hilary	Oliver	Saxon
Horace	Oswald	Sefton
Horatio	Pelham	Selwyn
Hugh	Peregrine	Tancred
Hugo	Philip	Valentine
Ivo	Quentin	Vere
James	Quintin	Vivian
Jermyn	Ralph	William
Julius	Randolph	

Proactive Names

The skinny culture of the Eighties is alive and kicking in the Nineties. Bodies are no longer things we go around in because we haven't got anything better. Now we actually enjoy them. More philosophical than physical, the honing-and-toning cult has evolved from lifestyle into way-of-life. Leaner, fitter, greener, it creates Proactives to whom life is a contact sport. They're Reeboks-with-attitude, outgoers and outdoers, sassy, sappy, and ozone-chummy; they're intelligent but not introspective, successful without taking work too seriously. Proactives have jaunty, up-beat names with a spring in the step.

OUTDOOR GIRLS

Ali	Holly	Nellie
Amy	Jamie	Patsy
Annie	Jody	Patti
Barbie	Josie	Peggy
Bella	Judi	Penny
Bessie	Kelly	Pippa
Betsy	Kerry	Polly
Bonny	Kiri	Poppy
Carly	Kirstie	Rosie
Carrie	Kitty	Rudy
Cindy	Laurie	Sally
Cody	Lucy	Shelley
Debbie	Maggie	Stacey
Dodie	Maisie	Suzi
Evie	Marcy	Tammy
Fifi	Merry	Trixie
Ginny	Millie	Trudi
Haidee	Mimi	Vicki
Heidi	Molly	Winnie

SWOT-SPOT

- Live Aider Bob Geldof has called one of his bouncing babies Fifi Trixiebelle, while Roger Daltrey went green with Rosie Lea; Moonlighter Cybill Shepherd stays up late with proactive Molly, and John 'Cougar' Mellencamp keeps on his toes with hyperactive Teddi-Jo.

LIVELY LADS

Barney	Jerry	Perkin
Billy	Jock	Ricky
Bo	Joey	Robbie
Brady	Josh	Rocco
Cappi	Judd	Sammy
Charlie	Kit	Terry
Chik	Leo	Theo
Eddie	Lucio	Toby
Fitz	Marco	Todd
Fritz	Mario	Vito
Gus	Max	Willie
Hal	Merryn	Zack
Harry	Nico	Zak
Jack	Otto	Zed
Jake	Paddy	Zig
Jamie		

SWOT-SPOT

- Four Basque brothers from Bilbao have been named
  alliteratively and athletically: Que Sevaya, Que Sevanga,
  Que Sesuba, and Que Sebaya. The translation? 'Come
  Here!', 'Go Away!', 'Go Up!', and 'Go Down!'.

Boss-Names

'Congratulations, it's a company director!' Some names carry exactly the right weight of authority and reliability to take a baby from the cot to the top. Boss-babes need names which won't lose balance when the prefix 'Judge', 'Sir' or 'Dame' is pinned to their pinstripes in later life. The Boss image is effective and forceful, always in control without being threatening. Rambosity and bimbosity are way off the agenda: for Boss-Woman, frills and frivolities are OUT; for Boss-Man, poker-faced neutralities are IN.

BOSS-WOMEN

Alison	Gail	Lynn
Anne	Gemma	Margaret
Bernice	Geraldine	Margery
Bridget	Gina	Margot
Carol	Gwen	Marian
Christine	Hannah	Marie
Claire	Harriet	Nicola
Clare	Helen	Paula
Cora	Janet	Pauline
Corinne	Janine	Rachel
Cynthia	Jean	Rebecca
Dorothy	Jill	Roisin
Emma	Joan	Rosa
Eve	Joanna	Ruth
Felicity	Joyce	Sarah
Fiona	Julie	Sian
Frances	Kate	Susan
Frieda	Louise	Veronica

BOSS-MEN

Adrian	Antony	Christopher
Alan	Benedict	Clive
Alexander	Bernard	Daniel
Alistair	Charles	David

BOSS-MEN

Dermot	Hamish	Oliver
Dominic	Henry	Patrick
Douglas	Hugh	Paul
Edward	Ian	Peter
Euan	Ivor	Philip
Frank	James	Richard
Frederick	John	Robert
Geoffrey	Laurence	Simon
George	Matthew	Stephen
Gerald	Michael	Thomas
Graham	Nicholas	William

Creative Names

Is it a Mona? Is it a Lisa? You can't teach creativity – but you *can* fan the flames by pouring gasoline on the merest wink of its divine spark. Creative names make heroes and princesses of every child who can carry them off with style. Names to dress up in, all teeth and eyes for those creative kids who can be relied upon to make a drama out of any crisis. Okay, they'll give you years of tantrums and stage fright instead of growing pains; they'll have Tate-a-Tates with you in place of mother–daughter chats. They'll make you laugh, they'll make you cry, they'll make you wait. But they'll be worth it. Applause. Applause. Applause.

PRIMA DONNAS

Adriana	Flavia	Meriel
Alethea	Flora	Minerva
Alfreda	Freya	Miranda
Allegra	Fulvia	Morgana
Anaïs	Germaine	Nyssa
Anthea	Giselle	Ophelia
Arden	Griselda	Oralia
Aretha	Grizel	Oriana
Ariadne	Guinevere	Paloma
Ariel	Hermia	Persephone
Astra	Hermione	Petra
Astrid	Iola	Phaedra
Aurora	Iphigenia	Phemie
Calypso	Isadora	Phoebe
Camille	Isolde	Portia
Cassandra	Jocasta	Psyche
China	Leonora	Rae
Chloris	Lilliana	Raphaela
Columbine	Lucasta	Ricarda
Delphina	Luciana	Richenda
Demetria	Maia	Richmal
Diantha	Margaux	Tamara
Eden	Maude	Venetia
Eldora	Melina	Vita
Electra	Melinda	

SWOT-SPOT

- A lovely name, Jocasta. But *do* avoid complexity by remembering that she was dear little Oedipus's mother!

PRINCIPAL BOYS

Amadeus	Felix	Lucian
Ambrose	Flavian	Luke
Anselm	Fletcher	Marcus
Anton	Florian	Marius
Auberon	Gabriel	Max
Aubrey	Harlequin	Orlando
Barnaby	Hector	Oscar
Ben	Inigo	Piers
Bertrand	Jago	Raphael
Byron	Jasper	Remus
Clovis	Julius	Riordan
Crispian	Justin	Rudyard
Cyprian	Kit	Sebastian
Darius	Leo	Titus
Dorian	Liam	Toby
Fabian	Lucas	Tristan

Wannabees

Babes on Top

When I Grow up I Wannabee . . .

When you gaze adoringly down at that helpless little bundle of naked ambition, don't you wanna know what it's gonnabee? Help is at hand with this home-testing kit. Compare your baby with the following descriptions – if one matches, you have a get-up-and-go wannabee who's already decided on a career but can't find the words to tell you.

Little Lawyer

If your baby has curly hair, an ever-open mouth, waves its arms about, makes constant appeals and prefers briefs to Pampers, then it's definitely a son or daughter in law.

GIRLS	BOYS
Aminta – protector	**Adlai** – witness
Brenna – raven	**Brock** – old badger
Calypso – concealer	**Calvin** – bald
Clementine – merciful	**Crispin** – curly-locks
Elfreda – wise counsellor	**Dempster** – the judge
Griselda – grey heroine	**Ewing** – friend of law

Baby Doc

Good cotside manners, warm hands, and a tendency to gurgle something not unadjacent to 'Aaargh' suggests a GP in the making. The swearing of Hippocratic oaths at the top of tiny lungs when you're late for any appointment completes the diagnosis.

you're overworked, doctor...

A L T H E A

GIRLS	BOYS
Adelphia – sisterly	**Asa** – healer
Althea – healer	**Blade** – rich. From surgery?
Anstice – resurrection	**Boniface** – worker of good
Bena – wise woman	**Canute** – knot. Tourniquet?
Buena – good woman	**Clay** – A plaster-caster?
Cassandra – get a second opinion!	**Corwin** – friend of the heart
Charity – love	**Hyman** – life
Hope	**Jason** – healer
Horatia – up-all-hours	**Lazarus** – God will help

Proto-Politician

This baby's always on its feet trying to catch your eye. It talks complete rubbish all the time, never gives Yes for an answer and never takes No for one. But its constitution is very sound and it debates happily with Teddy and Fluffy Rabbit.

GIRLS	BOYS
Abra – mother of multitudes	**Aldrich** – old ruler
Alarice – ruler of all	**Alvin** – friend of all
Basilia – queenly	**Campbell** – crooked mouth
Belinda – snake-like	**Leopold** – people's lion
Eulalia – fair-spoken	**Lysander** – the liberator
Luella – the appeaser	**Rex** – king
Margaret – iron-lady	**Sheridan** – wild savage
Radmilla – worker-for-the-people	**Todd** – the fox
Regina – queen	**Ulric** – ruler of all
Rula – sovereign	

Cub Reporter

This little chatterbox rattles out tittle-tattle at the going rate. It drinks an awful lot. It won't eat anything that isn't hot, spicy, and full of titbits. It begs you for a story but you don't get far. It always wants to hold the front page.

GIRLS	BOYS
Alethea – truth	**Abel** – breath
Aloha – greetings	**Angelo** – messenger

GIRLS	BOYS
Alpha – first	**Argus** – many-eyed
Angela – messenger	**Boden** – herald
Angharad – shameless	**Botolf** – herald-wolf
Annunciata – news-bearer	**Cameron** – crooked nose
Atalya – the Guardian	**Chase** – the hunter
Bernice – the Herald	**Chauncey** – recorder
Evangeline – bringer of good news	**Dennis** – wine-lover
Horatia – keeper of the Times	

Budding Farmer

Manure. Lots of it. This baby's a hardcore muck-spreader. Ruddy-faced and wholesome, it wears bootees and dungarees. It gets up at cockcrow. At breakfast, it waves a tiny pitchfork and a little shovel. It will eat organic food – so much quicker to recycle!

GIRLS	BOYS
Eartha – of the earth	**Carswell** – cress-grower
Gaea – earth-goddess	**Cicero** – chickpea
Georgina – farm-girl	**Laird** – landowner
Glenna – from the valley	**Latham** – from the barn

Toy Soldier

It's still too young to have enemies, but none of its friends like it. No sir! It lines up the teddies and shouts at them. It cuts the pom-pom off its hat to make a woolly beret. It sleeps with one eye open and the other hidden in its sock. It's Mummy's brave little soldier.

GIRLS	BOYS
Bernia – angel in armour	**Cadell** – battle-spirit
Berthilda – warrior-maid	**Cadman** – battle man
Brunhilda – iron maiden	**Frick** – bold man
Erma – army maid	**Garrett** – warrior
Gertrude – spearwoman	**Gawain** – battle-hawk
Gunhilda – warrior woman	**Guthrie** – war-snake
Haralda – army ruler	**Harald** – commander

Born Banker

Buy-Buy Baby. It counts its fingers. It counts its toes. It counts Teddy's fingers and Teddy's toes. It draws chalkstripes on its rompers. This little piggy is definitely going to market.

GIRLS	BOYS
Ada – prosperous	**Edmund** – rich guardian
Antonia – beyond price	**Felix** – fortunate
Aurelia – golden	**Franklin** – freeholder
Beverley – ambitious one	**Frey** – god of wealth
Daria – wealthy queen	**Prospero** – successful
Riccadonna – rich lady	**Ricco** – rich

Sex

From Rambo to Bimbo

I Love It When You Call me Names

Sex. The core of existence. Life's central mystery. And most of it's fun. All the best bits are naughty. In an earlier chapter, we looked at images which might give children an edge in daily life. Now we can chuck all that away and concentrate on night-life. Sex. Leap out of the boardroom and into bed.

For generations, parents have worried about whether their sons would marry a good dowry and whether their daughters would spark up a noble match. But nowadays it's up to the kids. As parents, you can help your child acclimatise to the demands of modern relationships by giving them good-looking names. But choose with meticulous care: sexual identity is painfully close to the heart.

He or She?

Most names say what sex you are. Many are decisively feminine or masculine. Between these extremes can be found sexual identities which sound less certain, and at the heart of the gender blur, where little wimmin meet wimps, lie the unisex names, definite only in their ambivalence.

A Boy Named Sue

Once it was alright to give a girl a girly name and a boy a boyish one. But nowadays women are a force in the workplace and men have been softened into New Man. It's a shift which permits parents to name female babies not just for prettiness but for power, to name boy babies not just for power but for sweetness and light. Women's annexation of male territory is greatest in America where there's been an epidemic of giving girls boys' names: Brookes, Kirbys, Whitneys and Courtneys abound in fe-male chauvinist pigtails. And when girls borrow boys' names, like their rugby shirts, they tend to keep them. But the boys don't want them back. They've gone too girly for that.

When he starts school, little boy Beverley won't blow you kisses. Remember, names remain in the vanguard of the battle of the sexes, so it's worth taking trouble over the sexual image your choice will project.

Sugar or Spice?

Names can't make you sexy. But they can make you *sound* sexy, which is half the battle, and make others *believe* it, which is the other half. Names are deeply suggestive. Isn't Calypso more blindly datable than dowdy old Morag? Isn't Gabriella more kissable than Oona? Here's a Girl Guide to who's who in sexual relativity:

Fem-Fatale – the voluptuous vamp
Femette – the baby-doll cuticle
Fem – the no-fuss all-rounder
Tomboy – the girls-on-top go-getter

Fem-Fatale

She's a sexually potent Black Widow. This gorgeous cannibal always gets her man. On toast for breakfast. Armed with nothing but a toothbrush, you'll find her clubbing the tropical moonlight away with European princelings given to the exotic. Extravagant in all her appetites, she keeps drooling admirers on a string as a head-hunter might keep scalps. But this volcanic Fem-Fatale's real lust is for life.

Acacia	Ambrosine	Aurora
Adora	Andromeda	Azura
Africa	Angelica	Bellina
Allegra	Astrid	Bianca
Amber	Atlanta	Brigitte

Calypso	Karina	Raquel
Candice	Lara	Rhea
Caprice	Larissa	Rochelle
Cara	Leila	Roma
Carlotta	Leonie	Rosalba
Cleopatra	Letitia	Rosetta
Coralie	Lola	Rufina
Damaris	Lolita	Sabra
Deanna	Lotus	Saffron
Delilah	Loveday	Salome
Desiree	Lucretia	Sapphira
Diva	Lydia	Savannah
Dominique	Madonna	Scarlett
Doria	Margarita	Seraphina
Ebony	Marietta	Serena
Elysia	Marina	Sibylla
Fawn	Melantha	Storm
Florinda	Melissa	Tamara
Galiena	Melita	Tanya
Georgia	Mia	Tara
Giselle	Miranda	Tatiana
Gloria	Nerissa	Titania
Gloriana	Odessa	Tiziana
Godiva	Olympia	Valentina
Isadora	Oriana	Venetia
Isis	Pandora	Venus
Ivory	Pleasance	Violante
Jessamine	Raphaela	Zinnia
Jezebel		

Femette

Sweetly pretty, more bland than blonde, the Femette seems destined more for the bedroom than the boardroom. But she'll marry the boss! She's often shrewdly intelligent under all those curls, but she hides it cleverly in gingham and giggles. She's sunny and sexy, keeping a neat house behind the net curtains. She adores anything coquettish, and her bimbo rating is far higher than her IQ. The Femette doesn't have a nasty bone in her body. Or a spine. But *don't* judge by appearance or underestimate her just because she gets her own way without hurting people: pretty, pleasant and popular, the Femette is nobody's fool!

Adrienne	Cherie	Genevieve
Alyssa	Cherry	Georgette
Amy	Cheryl	Gillian
Angela	Claribel	Haidee
Anita	Claudette	Hazel
Annabel	Colleen	Heather
Annette	Crystal	Hyacinth
April	Daisy	Isabella
Averil	Dawn	Jacquetta
Barbie	Donna	Jeanette
Bella	Dulcibella	Josette
Belle	Fay	Joy
Blossom	Fifi	Judy
Bonny	Fleur	Kirsty
Carla	Flora	Kitty
Cecily	Gabrielle	Lynette

Maisie	Nanette	Rosabel
Maria	Nerys	Samantha
Marigold	Nicole	Suzette
Mary	Nicolette	Tiffany
Melanie	Pamela	Tracy
Melody	Pansy	Violetta
Merry	Paulette	Vivienne
Mirabel	Prima	Yasmine
Monique	Renata	Yvette
Nancy	Renee	

Fem

Well-made and attractive, the Fems take everything in their stride. Romance and exaggerated sexuality are not for them. They are very female without being ultra-feminine, soft and caring but reliable in all weathers. Fem names are pretty in pillow-talk yet sound capable at work and pleasing at parties. Straight-talking and self-confident, many Fems feature among the **Classy Classics** and **Evergreens**. They remain a good but unfashionable bet for the no-fuss Nineties.

Abigail	Beatrice	Celia
Adelaide	Bridget	Clarissa
Aileen	Bronwyn	Clementina
Angela	Caitlin	Cordelia
Antonia	Candida	Cornelia
Audrey	Carola	Daphne
Barbara	Cecile	Deborah

Deirdre	Lilian	Rebecca
Delia	Linda	Rita
Dorothy	Liza	Rosalind
Eileen	Lorraine	Rosalyn
Eleanor	Louisa	Rosamond
Eliza	Madeleine	Rosaria
Emily	Margery	Rowena
Eva	Margot	Sara
Francine	Martina	Selina
Gwendolyn	Megan	Sheila
Harriet	Molly	Sonia
Helen	Monica	Sophie
Holly	Nadine	Susannah
Imogen	Naomi	Suzanne
Ingrid	Natalie	Sylvia
Isabel	Nina	Teresa
Jacqueline	Olivia	Therese
Janine	Patricia	Valerie
Jenna	Paula	Veronica
Jennifer	Pauline	Viola
Jessica	Penelope	Violet
Joanna	Philippa	Virginia
Juliet	Phyllida	Wendy
Kathleen	Polly	Yvonne
Lauren	Rachel	Zoe

Tomboys

Arguably, it is useful for the thoroughly modern missie to have a sex-free PC name about which there can be no Ms-take. But you don't have to win *Mastermind* to recognise that a child slowly discovering itself deserves a name with a clear sexual identity. So think carefully before you confuse your Issue. This said, tough-talk names don't *have* to be unisex. But they must play down femininity or offer scope for a boyish nickname. Tomboys are frank and unthreatening, good team-players and kindly confidantes. They take the lead in all areas, climbing life's ladder as nimbly as they once climbed trees.

Alex (andra)	**Chris** (tine)	**Kay**
Alexis	**Clem** (entine)	**Kim**
Ali (son)	**Cody**	**Kirby**
Alix	**Dale**	**Lesley**
Ariel	**Evelyn**	**Lindsay**
Ash	**George** (ina)	**Mo** (Maureen)
Ashley	**Gerry** (Geraldine)	**Patrice**
Beverley	**Henri** (etta)	**Robin**
Billie	**Hilary**	**Rudy**
Bo	**Jan** (ice)	**Sandy**
Brooke	**Jerry**	**Terry**
Cass (andra)	**Jo** (sephine)	**Vivien**

SWOT-SPOT

- In the Middle Ages, many blue-rinsed women were called Gilbert, Reynold, Basil, Giles, Edmund, Simon and Eustace.

- Before the Reformation, it was quite usual to name children with mauve names referring to their birthday – Christmas, Nowell, Easter, Pask, Whitsun, Pentecost, Epiphany, and Loveday.

- Lord Anne Hamilton was a posh cross-dresser, named after his godmother Queen Anne. Also in the pink, an early East Anglian ruler was called King Anna. English Roman Catholics sometimes christen a boy Mary after the Continental fashion honouring the Blessed Virgin.

- Alice, Crystal, Emma, Esme, Florence, Kimberley, Lucy and Maud were originally men's names.

- Muscular Christian was once a girl's name. And so was tough-guy Douglas.

- Back in 1932, a law was passed in Czechoslovakia banning the name Maria for boy babies on the grounds that names should state clearly a person's sex.

- George Eliot was the pen-name of Mary Anne Evans.

Slugs or Snails?

Boys' names come with a Rambosity rating. When flicking through this guide, bear in mind that it's probably worse for a man to have a too-butch or a too-fluffy name than it is for his sister to have an overly feminine or a neuter one. The male ego is a fragile thing which can get some ungentle strip-teasing in the football showers or in the Parachute Regiment. Here's a guide that sorts out the men from the boys:

Bov – the big-mac beefcake
Husky – the clean-cut classic
Hugger – the lead-free liberal
Woggle – the wimpish weakling

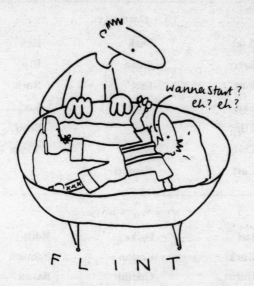

Bovs

Boys will be boys. Unfortunately, some boys will be Bovs, and they'll always cause bovver. As a breed, the Bovs are bikers and truckers, the spit-and-sawdust psychos, the sweaty string-vested superjocks. These men keep Rottweilers called Kill. They don't eat quiche. They can't even spell it. Bovs have tattoos, flexi-pex, and they give you heavy metal fatigue. Due to changing fashion, these bovine bozos appear in two lists, but all are appropriate for boys with the swinging blue genes of Tarzan on steroids.

- Og, the King of Basham – no, not Bash'em – was killed by Moses as he was throwing a mountain at the Israelites.

OLD-TIME BOVS

Axel	Dirk	Rex
Barry	Duke	Rip
Burt	Earl	Rock
Carl	Flint	Rod
Clint	Kev	Scott
Craig	Kirk	Vince
Curt	Rambo	

NEW-WAVE BOVS

Bart	Fulke	Rollo
Brock	Griffin	Samson
Brutus	Griffith	Saxon
Chad	Hugo	Sholto
Clay	Jago	Storr
Dax	Jock	Thor
Dolph	Quinn	Thorkell
Drogo	Rafe	Titus
Fitz	Raoul	Wolf
Fritz	Raven	

SWOT-SPOT

- On Yer Bike! In 1991, at least two protocycling Hell's Cherubs were saddled with the name Harley by their biker parents. Whose surname is Davidson.

Huskies

Huskies come with tweeds and cords – and a retriever in whose company they'd like to bag a brace of grouse with a pair of Purdeys. Huskies eat roast beef. Drink whisky. Give up their seats. These true blues don't want a pink name, or one blurring into mauve; they think men should be gentlemen and that a woman's place is in the home. Kindly, faithful, soldierly, unimaginative, Huskies don't want to be thought intellectual or arty – they'd rather be outdoors.

Adrian	Frederick	Nigel
Alan	Geoffrey	Patrick
Albert	George	Paul
Alfred	Gerald	Peter
Andrew	Gordon	Philip
Antony	Gregory	Ralph
Arthur	Harold	Raymond
Bernard	Henry	Richard
Charles	James	Robert
Christopher	John	Roger
Conrad	Joseph	Roland
David	Malcolm	Simon
Denis	Mark	Stephen
Donald	Matthew	Stuart
Douglas	Michael	Thomas
Edward	Neil	Timothy
Frank	Nicholas	William

Huggers

The Hugger is New Man grown up. With the rough corners put back on. He's recovered a good deal of his masculinity since the Seventies – out of his platform boots, the Hugger is now well adjusted. He likes pink. He can actually *make* quiche. The Hugger doesn't patronise women and he doesn't like them to matronise him. He loves to cook. He likes to !$*£%! He's in at the birth. He's good, he's Green, and he knows his geography. Like where the G-spot is. Where to put the nappy. And how to find the drier. The Hugger's Rambosity-rating is thankfully nil, yet he offers X-rated sex plus the huggability of a SuperTed. A woman's man, a man's man, the expressive Hugger is firm favourite for the title Millenial Man.

Abel	Benjamin	Dominic
Adam	Bram	Dougal
Aidan	Brendan	Duncan
Alban	Brewster	Dunstan
Alexander	Bruno	Edmund
Ambrose	Calum	Fabian
Angus	Christian	Fabius
Augustine	Clay	Felix
Austin	Clement	Fergal
Barnaby	Crispian	Fergus
Barnard	Crispin	Fingal
Bartholomew	Cuthbert	Finn
Basil	Damian	Finnian
Bede	Dickon	Fletcher
Benedick	Digby	Frey
Benedict	Diggory	Gabriel

Gerard	Julius	Perseus
Giles	Justin	Pierre
Gus	Kit	Quentin
Guy	Linus	Raphael
Haakon	Lucas	Raven
Hal	Luke	Reynard
Hobart	Marcus	Rowan
Ivo	Maxwell	Rufus
Jack	Merlin	Rupert
Jago	Merryn	Sam
Jake	Nat	Sebastian
Jarvis	Ned	Silas
Jeremy	Oliver	Simm
Jerome	Ovid	Toby
Jonathan	Owen	Tristan
Josh	Pagan	Tristram
Judd	Peregrine	Tybalt
Julian	Perkin	

Woggles

Oh dear. Woggles are double-whammy wimboes. No wambosity-wating whatsoever. They're the butterfingers who get picked last for every team – and picked on first for everything else. Their shorts are too long. They lisp. They swot. Woggles may very well have a sex drive, but when Nature doled out testosterone, these little Oliver Twists were way down the queue. Somehow, Woggles always seem to end up doing marvellous work for local charities. With their pebble glasses, buck teeth and flares, they're as welcome at the Church Social as the bloke who turns wine into water.

Alvin	Egbert	Marlon
Arnold	Eustace	Marmaduke
Beverley	Evelyn	Marvin
Blair	Gaylord	Maurice
Brian	Gideon	Melvin
Bruce	Herbert	Mervyn
Byron	Horace	Mortimer
Carol	Hubert	Norbert
Cecil	Humphrey	Orville
Cedric	Irving	Oswald
Clarence	Irwin	Percival
Courtney	Jason	Reginald
Cyril	Keith	Rodney
Dale	Kelvin	Russell
Darren	Kermit	Selwyn
Darryl	Leon	Sidney
Denys	Leslie	Sylvester
Desmond	Lester	Troy
Dudley	Marion	Wayne

Time and Space

Naming the day

Magic Moments

The second your baby is born, the world changes forever. It's like the Butterfly Effect when a gorgeous iridescent honeysuckler claps its wings in Tokyo and causes a storm in New York. And so far this book has dealt with equipping your baby to make an effect – the right image for sex, for work, for play. But this section is just for you and your baby; it has nothing to do with image or pushing ahead in the eyes of a critical world. It's about that moment when all the clocks stop and your child is born, a unique life ready to take its personal place in the heart of your home.

All the names in this chapter are concerned with the time, the day and the season of your baby's birth, or its place in the family. As well as names which have a special hug for adopted babies, there are names for dawn, day and night children – and for greenhorns born in spring, for summer's hot dogs, for the corn-dollies of harvest-home, and for the icicles and popsicles of winter.

Numbering your Brood

Some parents like to give a name reflecting their baby's place in the pecking order of the brood; this custom, perhaps rather old-fashioned nowadays, goes back to the days of huge draughty families when a child was rarely seen, never heard, and had to look after Number One until it was fit to fly the coop.

GIRLS	BOYS
Alpha – First girl	**Primo** – First boy
Prima – First girl	**Secundo** – Second boy
Winona – First girl	**Secundus** – Second boy
Secunda – Second girl	**Tertius** – Third boy
Tertia – Third girl	**Delta** – Fourth boy

GIRLS

Delta – Fourth girl

Tessa – Fourth girl

Tessara – Fourth girl

Penthea – Fifth girl

Quinta – Fifth girl

Sexta – Sixth girl

Zeta – Sixth girl

Bathsheba – Seventh girl

Septima – Seventh girl

Octavia – Eighth girl

Nona – Ninth girl

Decima – Tenth girl

Dixie – Tenth girl

Medea – Middle girl

Messina – Middle girl

BOYS

Quinn – Fifth boy

Quintin – Fifth boy

Quintus – Fifth boy

Sextus – Sixth boy

Septimus – Seventh boy

Octavian – Eighth boy

Octavius – Eighth boy

Otto – Eighth boy

Decimus – Tenth boy

GIRLS	BOYS
Bambi – The baby	
Ultima – Last girl	**Ultimo** – Last boy
Meta – Ambition achieved!	
Solita – Only child	
Una – Only child	
Tammy – Twin	**Thomas** – Twin
Tamsin – Twin	
Thomasina – Twin	

Giving your Baby the Time of Day

Just as some parents like to remember the place of conception or birth with names like Chelsea and Savannah – though hopefully no child will go to school as Maurice Minor! – others like to recall the day or time of birth. Try:

Lundy – Monday (f & m)	**Frey** – Friday (m)
Tuesday – Tuesday (f & m)	**Freya** – Friday (f)
Kwakoa – Wednesday (m)	**Frideswide** – Friday (f)
Woden – Wednesday (m)	**Kwame** – Saturday (m)
Odin – Wednesday (m)	**Domenica** – Sunday (f)
Thor – Thursday (m)	**Dominic** – Sunday (m)
Thora – Thursday (f)	**Dominique** – Sunday (f)
Thorald – Thursday (m)	**Neda** – Sunday (f)
Thordis – Thursday (m)	**Maloney** – Sunday (m)
Friday – Friday (f & m)	

DAWN GIRLS	DAWN BOYS
Anastasia – resurrection	**Abel** – first breath
Anstice – resurrection	**Cadmus** – man from the East
Aurora – dawn	
Daisy – day's eye	**Gilbert** – bright promise
Danica – morning star	**Giles** – youthful
Dawn	**Hyman** – life
Hebe – youth	**Ninian** – full of life
Lark	**Placido** – calm
Levanna – sun of the dawn	**Rene** – reborn
Renata – reborn	**Vidal** – life
Rose	**Vitalis** – vital
Roxanne – dawn	**Vitus** – life
Serena – calm	**Vivian** – lively
Stacey – resurrection	
Vita – life	
Vivienne – life	
Zarah – brightness of dawn	
Zerlinda – beautiful dawn	
Zoe – life	
Zorina – the dawn	

DAY GIRLS	DAY BOYS
Aakash – sky	**Aidan** – little fiery one
Aileen – bright	**Brand** – firebrand
Apollonia – sunny	**Clarence** – bright
Bertha – bright	**Cuthbert** – bright
Candace – bright	**Huw** – fire
Elena – light	**Kanti** – sun's rays
Helen – light	**Lucas** – light
Lenore – light	**Lucian** – light
Lenora – light	**Lucius** – light
Lucasta – light	**Luke** – light
Lucille – light	**Nural** – born in daylight
Phaedra – bright one	**Samson** – child of sun
Rokeya – she rises on high	**Sinclair** – shining light

NIGHT GIRLS	NIGHT BOYS
Adriana – dark stranger	**Adrian** – dark stranger
Arianwen – silvery	**Badhur** – born at full moon
Asta – star	**Bertram** – brilliant raven
Branwen – lovely raven	**Bertrand** – bright raven
Brenna – raven	**Bran** – raven
Chandra – moon	**Caspar** – star-following king
Chausiku – night-born	**Corbett** – raven
Diana – moon-goddess	**Darcy** – dark man
Pamina – daughter of the Queen of the Night	

Seasonal Names

SPRING CHICKS . . .

Agnes – lamb

Amaryllis – clear stream

Anastasia – resurrection

Anstice – resurrection

Anthea – flowery

April

Cerelia – new corn

Chloe – spirit of young crops

Chloris – fresh and blooming

Clarinda – shining blossom

Conception – the beginning

Easter

Estrild – Easter-battle

Evelina – hazel

Evelyn – hazel

Flora – spirit of spring

Hazel

Hebe – youthful

Hyacinth – fragrant bloom

Ianthe – violet

Idonea – Norse spring goddess

Iola – violet mist

Iris – rainbow

Jacintha – hyacinth

Kelda – bubbling spring

Laverne – spring-like

May

Neoma – new moon

Pascal – Easter

Phyllida – leafy

Phyllis – leafy

Primavera – spirit of spring

Primrose – first rose

Rabia – spring

Rachel – lamb

Spring

Sun

Sunny

Sunshine

Verda – green

Viola

Violet

Zera – seed

Zoe – life

. . . AND SPRING BUCKS

Aries – the Ram

Evelyn – hazel

Owen – lamb

Pascal – Easter

Pentecost

Phoenix – life from ashes

Rene – rebirth

Sholto – the sower

Vernon – spring-like

Vidal – vital

Vitalis – life

Vitus – life

Vivian – full of life

SUMMERTIME PINKS . . .

Azalea

Azura – deep blue

Blossom

Bryony

Cherry

Chryseis – golden daughter

Chrysogon – golden one

Clematis

Cliantha – flower of glory

Clover

Clytie – sun-worshipping nymph

Electra – bright one

Elysia – heavenly

Emerald

Euclea – glory

Fleur

Florence – blossoming

Halcyone – kingfisher

June

Lala – tulip

Lani – sky

Lark

Lavender

Lilac

Lily

Linnia – lime-blossom

Magnolia

Marigold

Mariposa – butterfly

Mavis – songthrush

Melissa – honey-bee

Merle – blackbird

Ora – golden

SUMMERTIME PINKS

Oriana – golden one	**Poppy**
Pamela – all-honeyed	**Posy**
Pansy	**Pyrena** – fiery one
Philantha – flower-lover	**Rosalba** – white rose
Philomena – nightingale	**Sadira** – lotus-eater
Phoebe – shining one	**Sapphira** – deep blue

. . . AND SUMMERTIME BLUES

Arden – fiery one	**Julius**
Cyrus – sun-god	**Junius**
Fraser – strawberry-gatherer	**Orion** – son of light
Galvin – sparrow	**Phoebus** – sun-god
Halcyon – kingfisher	**Samson** – sun's child
Joubert – shining one	**Sol** – sun
Julian	**Somerset** – summer place
Julio	

FALL GIRLS . . .

Amber	**Gilda** – gold
Anona – harvest goddess	**Golda**
Avena – oatfield	**Goldie**
Bracken	**Heather**
Fern	**Leaf**
Fronde	**Pomona** – fruitful
Garnet – pomegranate	**Prunella** – plum-coloured
Genista – broom-flower	**Rowena**

FALL GIRLS

Ruby	Tempest
Rusty	Teresa – harvester
Saffron	Thora – thunder
Scarlett	Topaz
Sorrel	Willow
Storm	Zea – ripe grain

. . . AND FALL GUYS

Bruno – brown	Rowan
Edan – flame	Roy – red
Leif – beloved	Rufus – red
Reid – red	Russell – red
Reuben – red	Storm
Reynard – the fox	Thor – thunder-god
Rooney – red	

SNOWGIRLS . . .

Bianca – white	Josephine – may Jehovah increase
Blanche – white	Krystle
Christmas	Lalath – white
Crystal	Laura – evergreen
Hesper – evening-star	Laurel – evergreen
Holly	Lauren – evergreen
Iva	Leila – night
Ivy	

SNOW GIRLS

Lilith – lady of darkness

Mary

Melania – robed in darkness

Melantha – dark flower

Natalie – Christmas-born

Nebula – misty

Nicola – victory of the people

Nissa – Norse imp

Noelle – Christmas

Nordica – girl of the North

Pamina – daughter of Queen of the Night

Persephone – nether-goddess

Petrina – from the rock

Stephanie – crowned

Yule

Zilla – shadow

. . . AND SNOWMEN

Angelo – angel

Caspar – one of the three kings

Christmas

Flint

Garwood – from the firs

Grey

Jaspar – version of Caspar

Joseph – God will multiply

Nicholas – victory of the people

Noel

Revel – shepherd

Rock

Star

Stinson – son of stone

Wenceslaus – wreath, or king of that name

Yul

Yule

Adopted Names

The adopted baby is the most mysterious of all strangers.
Parents who have yearned for that precious bolt from the blue –
or the pink – may want to show their gratitude for the baby who
now embraces them. A thanks-offering name which goes
beyond Tom, Dick or Harriet. Goes even beyond our Ken.

Abebi – asked-for child (f)

Aduke – much-loved child (f)

Angus – the only choice (m)

Aspasia – welcome (f)

Desiderata – longed-for (f)

Desideratus – longed-for (m)

Desiree – desired (f)

Dieudonnee – God-given (f)

Donata – gift (f)

Donatus – gift (m)

Dora – gift of God (f)

Dorothy – gift of God (f)

Ediva – rich gift (f)

Fergus – choice of man (m)

Renata – reborn (f)

Rene – reborn (m)

Theodore – gift of God (m)

Literary Allusions

*Literary illusions and
poetic fallacies*

Literary Illusions and Poetic Fallacies

Many names now in common use were either made up by authors or brought into fashion by them. Some of the most notable are listed below.

Amanda – Appears to be a seventeenth-century invention, used by Vanbrugh for his heroine of 'The Relapse' (1697). It was further popularised by Noel Coward's 1930 play *Private Lives*.

Anthea – Feminine of the Greek word for 'flower' and used by seventeenth-century pastoral poets as a name.

Araminta – A literary concoction of the Restoration period, part of a revival of interest in the classical or pseudo-classical.

Candida – First real use dates from the 1898 publication of G.B. Shaw's *Candida*.

Cedric – Used by Sir Walter Scott in *Ivanhoe*, possibly in error for the Saxon 'Cerdic'. Became fashionable after the 1886 publication of *Little Lord Fauntleroy* whose name it was.

Clarinda – Coined by Spenser for *The Faerie Queen*.

Dawn – An invention of the twentieth century, appearing in a number of popular novelettes.

Deirdre – From an Irish name but brought into the mainstream as a feature of the turn-of-the-century Celtic Revival. Yeats, for example, used it for *Deirdre* and Synge for *Deirdre of the Sorrows*.

Doreen – An Irish folk heroine brought to mainland prominence through Edna Lyall's popular novel *Doreen* of 1894.

Dorinda – An eighteenth-century form of Dorothy given a plug by Farquhar's *The Beaux's Strategem* (1707).

Elaine – Not found as Christian name before Tennyson's *The Idylls of the King* (1859) brought the story of Lancelot and Guinevere to the public. The tales were originally from Malory's *Morte d'Arthur*.

Enid – A Welsh name given appeal by Tennyson's *The Idylls of the King*, containing 'Geraint and Enid' (1859).

Esmeralda – Spanish world for 'emerald', boosted when Victor Hugo used it for *The Hunchback of Notre Dame*.

Estelle – A corruption of the French word for 'star', made fashionable by Dickens's *Great Expectations* – in which Pip falls in love with Estella.

Evangeline – Invented by Longfellow for 'Evangeline' (1847).

Fenella – A variation of the Irish Fionnuala or Finola, introduced to Britain by Scott's *Peveril of the Peak*.

Fleur – French version of the name Flora brought to attention by John Galsworthy's *Forsyte Saga* (1926–30). Florinda, another literary form, was used by Southey for his 1814 *Roderick the Last of the Goths*.

Geraldine – Used by the Earl of Surrey to conceal the subject of his love poems (c. 1540), Lady Elizabeth Fitzgerald.

Imogen – Used by Shakespeare in *Cymbeline*. The name seems to be the result of a printer's error for the Innogen of Holinshed.

Lorna – Invented by R. D. Blackmore for the heroine of his 1869 blockbuster, *Lorna Doone*.

Lucasta – A conceit of Lovelace who used it as a poetical address for his mistress, believed to be a member of the Lucas family.

Lucinda – Seventeenth-century poetical variation of Lucy which caught on.

Mavis – An old name for the songthrush. Novelist Marie Corelli seems to have used it first for one of her characters.

Myra – Probably made up by Fulke Greville (1554–1628) who addressed a lady by it in his love poems.

Percival – Apparently created by Crestien de Troyes for the hero of his twelfth–century poem 'Percevale'.

Perdita – Coined by Shakespeare for *The Winter's Tale* – from the Latin 'perditus', meaning lost.

Thelma – Made up by Marie Corelli for the Scandinavian star of her book *Thelma: A Society Novel* (1887).

Vanessa – Swift's adaptation of Esther Vanhomrigh.

Wendy – Made up by J. M. Barrie for *Peter Pan*, from the pet name 'Friendy-Wendy', given to him by a child.

SHAKESPEARE'S SISTERS

Adriana	Helena	Miranda
Aemilia	Hermia	Mopsa
Audrey	Hero	Nerissa
Beatrice	Hippolyta	Octavia
Bianca	Imogen	Olivia
Blanche	Iris	Ophelia
Bona	Isabel	Patience
Calpurnia	Isabella	Perdita
Cassandra	Jaquenetta	Phebe
Charmian	Jessica	Phrynia
Cleopatra	Joan	Portia
Cordelia	Julia	Regan
Cressida	Juliet	Rosalind
Desdemona	Katherina	Rosaline
Dionyza	Lavinia	Silvia
Dorcas	Luce	Tamora
Eleanor	Lucetta	Thaisa
Francisca	Luciana	Timanara
Gertrude	Margery	Titania
Goneril	Mariana	Ursula
Helen	Marina	Viola

SHAKESPEAROES

Adam	Fabian	Orlando
Adriano	Ferdinand	Orsino
Alonzo	Feste	Osric
Angelo	Fleance	Oswald
Angus	Florizel	Othello
Antony	Frederick	Owen
Arthur	Gerrold	Pedro
Baptista	Griffith	Peto
Bardolph	Hal	Petruchio
Benedick	Hamlet	Prospero
Bertram	Horatio	Puck
Brutus	Iago	Quince
Caius	Jachimo	Reynaldo
Caliban	Jacques	Rinaldo
Casca	Julius	Romeo
Cassius	Laertes	Sampson
Cinna	Launcelot	Silvius
Claudio	Lear	Siward
Claudius	Lucio	Speed
Corin	Lysander	Timon
Cornelius	Malcolm	Titus
Curtis	Malvolio	Toby
Dion	Nym	Troilus
Duncan	Oberon	Tybalt
Edgar	Oliver	Valentine
Edmund		

Phantoms of the Opera: *Names to Hit the High Spots*

SOPRANOS

Adina	Elsa	Norma
Aida	Flora	Olga
Amelia	Floria	Olympia
Annina	Frasquita	Ortrud
Azucena	Giannetta	Senta
Barbarina	Gilda	Serena
Berta	Giulietta	Sophie
Bess	Jenufa	Stella
Brangane	Leonore	Susanna
Carmen	Marcellina	Tatiana
Despina	Marianne	Violetta
Dorabella	Marina	Xenia
Ellen	Micaela	

TENORS

Alfio	Figaro	Matteo
Balthasar	Florestan	Melot
Beppe	Friedrich	Oscar
Boris	Fyodor	Otello
Cesare	Gabriel	Rocco
Cherubino	Giorgio	Roderigo
Crespel	Jacquino	Ruiz
Cristian	Jake	Silvio
Daland	Jose	Tristan
Ferrando		

Taking our Names in Vain: *Nomenclature in Words and Phrases*

Alec – **'smart Alec'**, a would-be wit.

Alice – **'Alice blue'**, a colour named for Alice Roosevelt; **'Alice band'**, a ribbon worn by Alice in Tenniel's illustrations for *Through the Looking-Glass*, 1872.

Albert – **'Fat Albert'**, USAF slang for the Hercules plane.

Bertha – **'Big Bertha'**, great gun used in 1918 to shell Paris, named after Berta Krupp – erroneously, as Krupps had not actually made the gun!

Biddy – **'Old biddy'**, meaning elderly lady. Deriving from the common name Bridgid, it originally meant any Irishwoman.

Bill – **'Old Bill'**, the police; **'silly billy'**, a duffer; **'billy goat'**, a male goat; **'Billy Bunter'**, a fat person, from the character created by Frank Richards.

Bobby – **'bobby'**, a policeman, named after Sir Robert Peel who is credited with founding the police. First use, 1844.

Bob – **'Bob's your uncle!'**, expression meaning 'a neat result'.

Charles – **'Charles's wain'**, the seven bright stars of the Plough.

Charlie – **'a right Charlie'**, a fool; **'champagne Charlie'**, fun-loving high-liver.

Cissy – **'a cissy'**, a spineless or effeminate male, from Cecily.

Davy – **'Davy Jones'**, sailor's name for the malign spirit of the sea. Origin unknown.

Dick – **'dick'**, private detective; vulgar name for the penis; also **'dickhead'**, an idiot; **'clever dick'**, a smart-ass; **'dead-eyed dick'**, a good shot; **'tricky-dicky'**, a twister.

Dido – **'to act Dido'**, to play the fool.

Dorcas – **'Dorcas society'**, a sewing-circle of women making clothes for charity. Named for a Biblical character famed for her good works.

Dorothy – **'Dorothy bag'**, a handbag closed by drawstrings.

Ebenezer – **'ebenezer'**, a religious meeting-house – from the memorial stone set up by Samuel in the Bible.

Fanny – **'sweet Fanny Adams'**, meaning nothing, from a girl of that name murdered and chopped up c.1812; **'fanny'**, colloquial expression for female genitals.

George – Name for aircraft autopilot; **'by George'**, mild oath referring to the saint; **'geordie'**, a native of Tyneside and a miner's lamp named after its maker, George Stephenson.

Harry – **'Old Harry'**, the Devil; **'flash Harry'**, a spiv.

Harvey – **'Harvey Smith'**, obscene gesture – from the show-jumper of that name who used it during a contest; **'Harvey Wallbanger'**, a cocktail.

Heath – **'Heath Robinson'**, used adjectivally to describe mad-cap contraptions, from name of artist (1872–1944).

Hector – **'to hector'**, to bluster and bully – from the prince of Troy.

Henry – **'Hooray Henry'**, a loud yobbish upper-crust type

Jack – **'Black Jack'**, the pirate flag; **'blackjack'**, a short lead and leather club and also a card game; **'Union Jack'**, the British flag at sea; **'yellow jack'**, slang for yellow fever; **'Jack Frost'**, personification of winter; **'Jack Sprat'**, a small weedy man; **'Jack tar'**, a sailor, so named because seamen wore tarpaulin; **'every man jack'**, everyone; **'jack-of-all-trades'**, versatile but unspecialised hack; **'Jack-in-the-Green'**, the May king or Green Man, spirit of fertility; **'cheap jack'**, a pedlar of trash.

Jane – **'a jane'**, slang for a woman; **'plain Jane'**, a frumpy girl.

Jenny – **'a jenny'**, a generic term for a country girl.

Jessie – Insulting Scots term for effeminate man.

Jimmy – **'Jimmy Riddle'**, to urinate – possibly rhyming slang for 'piddle'.

Joan – **'Darby and Joan'**, devoted elderly couple from an eighteenth-century song.

Jock – **'Jock'**, a Scot; **'Jock Scott'**, an angling fly; **'sports jock'**, brainless brawny games fanatic.

Joe – **'Joe Miller'**, a stale old joke – derived from the famously dull comedian of that name, 1684–1738; **'Joey'**, a clown, from Joseph Grimaldi; **'Joe Soap'**, the sucker lumbered with the dirty jobs; **'GI Joe'**, the typical US soldier; **'Joe Public'**, the typical citizen; **'holy Joe'**, slang for priest; **'sloppy joe'**, a loose jersey.

John – **'Blue John'**, a type of fluorspar; **'John Barleycorn'**, the personification of malt liquor; **'John Bull'**, the generic Englishman, from Arbuthnott's 1712 *History of John Bull*; **'John Thomas'**, slang for penis; **'john'**, American colloquial for lavatory; **'johnny'**, condom; **'Johnny-come-lately'**, a newcomer or a novice.

Jonah – **'a jonah'**, a bringer of bad luck; **'jonah word'**, one which causes a stutterer difficulty.

Jonathan – **'Brother Jonathan'**, the collective people of the United States.

Larry – **'the Larries'**, Britain's Laurence Olivier Awards.

Lizzie – **'Busy Lizzie'**, an industrious person – and a plant of the *Impatiens* genus.

Mae – **'Mae West'**, an airman's pneumatic life-vest, named for its supposed resemblance to the film-star's figure.

Maria – **'Black Maria'**, a prison van.

Mary – **'Bloody Mary'**, a red cocktail, named for Mary Tudor.

Mick – Derogatory term for an Irishman; **'mickey finn'**, a doped drink; **'to take the mickey'**, to mock.

Mike – **'for the love of Mike'**, euphemism for God in an expression of exasperation.

Minnie – **'moaning minnies'**, expression of unknown etymology used by former British prime minister Margaret Thatcher to describe the Press.

Mercedes – Famous car company, named for the owner's daughter.

Moll – **'gangster's moll'**, generic term for an underworld girlfriend. Originally from Moll Cutpurse, the nickname of Mary Frith, a notorious criminal.

Nancy – **'nancy'**, **'nance'**, **'nancy-boy'**, **'Miss Nancy'**, insulting slang for effeminate or homosexual male; **'Nancy-pretty'**, the plant Saxifraga umbrosa, probably a corruption of 'none-so-pretty'.

Ned – **'Ned'**, Scots for hooligan; **'Neddy'**, a donkey.

Nelly – **'not on your Nelly!'** – originally 'Nelly Duff', this was rhyming slang for 'puff' – or life – and meant 'not on your life!'.

Nick – **'Old Nick'**, the Devil.

Paddy – Derogatory slang for an Irishman; **'in a paddy'** in a rage, probably from the Irish passion in debate.

Paul – **'a Paul Pry'**, a nosy person – from John Poole's 1825 play of that name.

Peter – **'Blue Peter'**, flag hoisted when ship about to sail – and a long-running children's television programme; **'Rob Peter to pay Paul'**, taking money from one to give to another; **'Peter's pence'**, cash given by Catholics to support the Vatican; **'for Pete's sake'**, an expression of anger, avoiding blasphemy.

Roger – **'Jolly Roger'**, the skull-and-crossbones flag; **'Roger'**, radio code for 'received'; **'rogering'**, coarse slang for sexual act.

Roland – **'a Roland for an Oliver'**, tit-for-tat, giving as good as you get, from the contest – a draw – between two comrades in the Charlemagne epic.

Sam – **'Sam Browne'**, an officer's belt and straps, named after General Sam Browne; **'Uncle Sam'**, the US Government; **'sammy'**, a US soldier.

Sandy – Generic name for a Scotsman.

Shamus – **'a shamus'**, a detective.

Simon – **'Simon Pure'**, the genuine article; **'simple Simon'**, a slow-witted fellow.

Tom – **'Tommy Atkins'**, generic term for British private; **'Peeping Tom'**, prurient watcher from the tale of Godiva; **'Old Tom'**, **'Tom Collins'**, cocktails; **'every Tom, Dick, and Harry'**, everybody; **'tommy-rot'**, rubbish.

Walter – **'Walter Mitty'**, an intrepid dreamer, from the short story by James Thurber; **'wally'**, a nerd.

Willy – **'a willy'**, slang, usually childish, for the penis.

Glossary of Girls' Names

Note The following abbreviations are used throughout the Glossary:

(Af) African
(Arab) Arabic
(Celt) Celtic
(Dan) Danish
(Eng) Modern English
(Fr) Modern French
(Ger) Modern German
(Gk) Greek
(Haw) Hawaiian
(Heb) Hebrew
(Irish) Irish Gaelic
(It) Italian
(Jap) Japanese

(Lat) Latin
(Native American) American Indian
(OE) Old English
(OF) Old French
(OG) Old German
(ON) Old Norse
(Pers) Persian
(San) Sanskrit
(Scot) Scots Gaelic
(Slav) Slavonic
(Sp) Spanish
(Welsh) Welsh

It's a girl!

A

Alexandra (GK) 'defender'. Also Alexandria   46, 66, 73, 99

Alison (OG) 'noble', French diminutive of Alice. Also Alicia   17, 38, 45, 46, 47, 70, 75, 78, 99, 128

Alix (Gk) Short form of Alexandra   99

Aliza (Heb) 'joy'   47

Allegra (It) 'lively'. The name of Lord Byron's daughter   64, 80, 94

Aloha (Haw) 'greetings'   87

Alpha (Gk) first   88, 109

Althea (Gk) 'healthy'   86

Alyssa (Gk) 'sensible'   96

Alyssum (Gk) 'sensible'. Sweet Alyssum is a delicate white-flowering plant   47

Amabel (Lat) 'lovable'. Mabel is the short form   17

Amalia (Lat) from the Roman clan Aemilius. Also Amalie   64

Amanda (Lat) 'lovable'. Probably a seventeenth-century invention   38, 46, 123

Amaryllis (Gk) 'fresh stream'. Classical poets used this name to describe a fresh country girl   114

Amber (Arab) petrified sap used as jewellery and believed to have curative properties. It became popular as a name with the 1950s book *Forever Amber*   55, 94, 116

Ambrosine (Gk) 'divine'   49, 94

Amelia (OG) 'industrious'   73, 127

Amethyst (Gk) 'intoxicated'. The purple crystal was called 'amethyst' because it was held to protect from the effects of drink   55

Amice (Lat) 'beloved'   49

Aminta (Lat) 'protector'   85

Amy (Lat) 'beloved'   17, 38, 75, 96

Anastasia (Gk) 'resurrection'   15, 62, 73, 112, 114

Andromeda (Gk) the beautiful princess rescued by Perseus from a sea-monster   94

Anemone (Gk) 'wind-flower'. A Greek nymph turned into a flower by the wind – or the flower springing from the blood of the handsome god Adonis, killed while hunting   56

Andra (ON) 'a breath'   60

Andrea (Gk) 'brave'. Feminine of Andrew   70

Angela (Gk) originally 'messenger', now 'angel'   88, 96, 97

Angelica (Gk) 'angelic one'. Used by Milton in 1671 for *Paradise Regained*   94

Angharad (Welsh) 'well-beloved'   60, 88

Aniela (Heb) 'graceful'. Polish form of Anna – and Italian form of Angela   62

Anita (Heb) 'graceful'. Spanish diminutive of Anna   41, 96

Anna (Heb) 'graceful'. Variation on the Hebrew Hannah   43, 70

Annabel (Lat/Fr) 'lovable'. A Scottish name known since the twelfth century and borne by the mother of James I   41, 96

Annalise (Ger) combination of Anna and Lisa   64

Anne (Heb) 'graceful'. Version of Hebrew Hannah. Anne is traditionally the mother of the Virgin Mary. Also Anezka, Ana, Anaïs   12, 45, 63, 64, 78, 80

Anneka (Heb) 'graceful'. Swedish diminutive of Anna   63

Annie (Heb) 'graceful'. Popular diminutive in the English-speaking world for Anne, now a name in its own right   43, 75

Annette (Heb) 'graceful'. French diminutive of Anne   96

Annina (Heb) 'graceful'. Uncommon diminutive of Anne   127

Annunciata (Lat) 'bearer of news'. A name given to

babies born in March, referring to the Feast of the Annunciation. Rare in Britain 88

Anona (Lat) 'annual crops' or 'ninth-born'. Also Nona 110, 116

Anstice (Gk) 'resurrection'. An English form of Anastasia 86, 112, 114

Anthea (Gk) 'flowery' 56, 80, 114, 123

Antigone (Gk) The tragic, heroic daughter of King Oedipus

Antoinette (Lat) French diminutive form of Antonia

Antonia (Lat) 'priceless'. Feminine form of Roman Antonius 73, 89, 97

Antonina (Lat) 'priceless'. Diminutive of Antonia 62

Aphrodite (Gk) Goddess of love, a common name in Greece 65

Apollonia (Gk) 'from Apollo', of the sun-god 113

April (Lat) 'opening', 'spring'. Now, the month April 96, 114

Arabella (Lat) 'lovable'. A Scottish name, dating from the twelfth century, Latinised in the eighteenth-century 15, 73

Araminta (Lat) 'loving'. A seventeenth-century literary invention 73, 123

Arden (OE) 'eagle-valley'. Shakespeare's magical forest 80

Aretha (Gk) 'virtue' 80

Ariadne (Gk) 'very holy one'. Princess of Crete who helped Theseus fox the Minotaur and escape the labyrinth 49, 80

Ariana (Gk) Latin version of Ariadne 63

Ariane (Gk) French version of Ariadne, used for the pan-European space rocket programme 64

Arianwen (Welsh) 'silver-white' 113

Ariel (Heb) One of the names of God. In Shakespeare's *The Tempest*, Ariel is the quicksilver spirit who serves Prospero on the island 80, 99

Ashley (OE) 'from the ash-tree meadow'. A name made popular by *Gone with the Wind* (1936). The name and its short form, Ash, are used for both sexes 99

Asia (Lat) The continent 66

Aspasia (Gk) 'welcome'. The mistress of Pericles, architect of the golden age of Athens 119

Asphodel (Gk) 'asphodel-flower'. The flowers were said to bloom in Elysium, the ancient Greek heaven 49

Asta (Gk) 'star' 113

Astra (Lat) 'star' 80

Astrid (Gk) 'star'. Also, 'divine-strength' in Norse, via Old German 63, 80, 94

Atalya (Sp) 'guardian' 88

Athena (Gk) 'wisdom'. Pallas Athena was the goddess of Wisdom, represented by an owl 65

Atlanta (Gk) 'swift runner'. In Greek myth, Atlanta – or Atalanta – would only marry a man who could outsprint her. Also a place name 94

Audrey (OE) 'noble-strength' 6, 70, 97, 125

Augusta (Lat) 'venerable'. Roman title for imperial ladies, revived in Britain by the Hanoverians 4

Aurea (Lat) 'golden' 49

Aurelia (Lat) 'golden'. Feminine form of a noble Roman family 4, 15, 47, 89

Auriol (Lat) 'golden'

Aurora (Lat) 'dawn'. Aurora was the goddess of the dawn in Roman mythology 47, 80, 94, 112

Avalon (Lat) 'island'. In Celtic mythology, the island paradise where King Arthur and his knights sleep

Averil (OE) 'boar-battle' 96

Avice (OG) 'sanctuary-in-war'. Or, 'bird', from the Latin 9

Azalea (Gk) 'parched'. The highly scented azalea shrub which thrives in the driest soil, producing rich blooms 56, 115

Azura (Pers) 'lapis-lazuli blue'. Lapis lazuli is an azure-coloured stone ground to a heavenly blue dye and much used by the ancient Egyptians   94, 115

B

Bambi (It) 'the baby'. Also Bambalina, 'little child'   111

Barbara (Gk) 'foreigner'   8, 97

Barbarina (Gk) Diminutive of Barbara   127

Barbie (Gk) Short form of Barbara, now with rather bimbo-esque connotations   75, 96

Barbra (Gk) Danish form of Barbara   39

Basilia (Gk) 'queenly'. Rare feminine of Basil, 'kingly' 49, 87

Bathsheba (Heb) 'daughter of an oath', or 'seventh daughter'. Bathsheba was the mother of Solomon   13, 110

Beatrice (Lat) 'bringer of happiness'. Used as Dante's unattainable ideal of love in *The Divine Comedy* and as a Shakespeare character in *Much Ado About Nothing*   12, 43, 73, 97, 125

Beatrix (Lat) 'bringer of happiness'   49, 73

Belinda (OG) 'snake-like'; snakes were once revered as sacred   46, 87

Bella (It) 'beautiful'   75

Belle (Fr) 'beautiful'   96

Bellina (It) 'beautiful'   94

Bena (Heb) 'wise'   86

Berengaria (OG) 'bear-spear'. Wife of the glamorous crusader Richard I, known as Richard the Lionheart   49

Berengiere (OG) French form of Berengaria   49

Berenice (Gk) 'victory-bringer'. Also Bernice and Bernita   78, 88

Bernadette (OG) 'resolute as a bear'. Feminine of Bernard

Berta (OG) 'illustrious'. Also Bertha   9, 63, 70, 113, 127, 128

Berthilda (OE) 'shining battle-maid'. Also Bertilde 89

Beryl (Gk) 'sea-green crystal'. Implies precious clarity 58

Bess (Heb) 'God is my satisfaction'. English familiar of Elizabeth. Also Bessie, Beth, Betsy, Bettina and Betty 43, 75, 127

Beulah (Heb) 'married, matronly, motherly'

Beverley (OE) 'from the beaver-meadow' 41, 89, 99

Bianca (It) 'white' 39, 94, 117, 125

Billie (OE) 'determination'. Also a short form of Wilhelmina 99

Blanca (Sp) 'white' 64

Blanche (Fr) 'white' 70, 117, 125

Blaze (OE) 'fiery torch'. Also Blaise and Blasia 49

Blodwen (Welsh) 'white flower' 60

Blossom (OE) blossom 56, 96, 115

Blythe (OE) 'gentle, joyful'. Also Blisse and Bliss

Bona (Ar) 'builder' 125

Bonita (Lat) 'good'; Spanish 'pretty' 49

Bonnie (Lat) 'good'; Scots dialect, 'pretty'. Also Bonny 39, 75, 96

Bracken (Eng) 'bracken' 116

Brangane (Welsh) 'white raven' 127

Branwen (Welsh) 'beautiful raven' 113

Brenda (ON) 'torch'. Feminine form of the Norse name Brand. A Shetland Isles name, its popularity was spread by Sir Walter Scott's use of it in *The Pirate* of 1822. Given commonly, but mistakenly, as a female version of Brendan 6, 60

Brenna (Irish) 'raven' 85, 113

Bridget (Irish) 'mighty one', the name of the Old Irish goddess of fire. Bridget is the English form of the Irish Brigid. Other forms: Biddy, Birgitta, Brigitta, and Brigitte 60, 64, 78, 94, 97, 128

Britannia (Lat) the name given by the Romans to Britain, used as a name in the eighteenth-century 49

Britta (Irish) Version of Brigid. Also Britt, a Scandinavian form   63

Brittany (Lat) Name of region of northern France   66

Bronwen (Welsh) 'white breast'. Also Bron and Bronwyn   60, 70, 97

Brooke (OE) 'from the brook'. A surname adopted as an ambisexual first name. Also Brook   99

Brunella (OF) 'brown-haired'. Also Brunetta   49

Brunhilda (OG) 'breastplate of battle'. In a Norse/German legend made famous by Richard Wagner's opera cycle *The Ring*, Brunhilda was one of the warrior-nymphs of Valhalla, the Valkyrie. Also Brunilla, Brynhild, and Hilda   49, 89

Bryna (Irish) 'strength-honour'   60

Bryony (English) An English hedgerow plant   56, 115

C

Caitlin (OF) Irish/Gaelic form of Catherine   97

Calandra (Gk) 'lark'. Also Calandria   49

Calpurnia (Gk) 'beautiful lady-of-the-night'. In Shakespeare's *Julius Caesar*, Calpurnia is Caesar's wife   4, 125

Calypso (Gk) 'concealer'. In Homer's epic *The Odyssey*, Calypso was the beautiful sea-nymph whose charms kept Odysseus prisoner on her island   49, 80, 85, 95

Camellia (Lat) Beautiful blooming shrub, named for its finder Camellus   56

Camilla (Lat) 'attendant at sacrifice'. Also Camille   64, 73, 80

Candace (Lat) 'shining white'. Also Candia, Candice, Candida, Candide   49, 73, 95, 97, 113, 123

Caprice (Lat) 'impulsive'   95

Cara (Lat) 'beloved'. Also Carina, Carita, Kara   95

Carla (OG) 'womanly'. Italian feminine version of Charles   96

Carlotta (OG) 'womanly'. Italian feminine diminutive of Charles. Also Carly   39, 64, 75, 95

Carmel (Heb) 'garden'. Also Carmela, Carmelina, Carmelita   65

Carmen (Heb) 'garden'. Also Carma, Carmencita, Carmina, Carmine, Carmita, Charmaine   127

Carol (OG) 'womanly'. A female form of Charles, Carol is regarded as a short form of Caroline not given to girls before the twentieth century   41, 76

Carola (OG) 'womanly'. A rare feminine form of Charles, derived from the Latin Carolus   15, 73, 97

Carolina (OG) Italian diminutive of Carola imported to England in the French form, Caroline. Also Carolyn, Carrie   46, 66, 73, 75

Cassandra (Gk) The name of the prophetess daughter of King Priam of Troy, destined never to have her prophecies believed. Also Cass, Cassia, Cassie   47, 73, 80, 86, 99, 125

Catalina (Gk) 'pure'. A version of Catherine   66

Catherine (Gk) 'pure'   12, 38, 45, 70

Cecilia (Lat) 'blind'. Latinised form of the English mediaeval Cecily   46, 70

Cecily (Lat) 'blind'. Deriving from the Roman gens, Caecilius, the name was given by William the Conqueror to one of his many daughters. Also Celia, Cecile, Cicely, Cissie   9, 43, 45, 64, 96, 97, 128

Celandine (Gk) 'swallow'. Also the name of a pretty yellow flower which comes with snowdrops in the first suns of spring   56

Celeste (Lat) 'heaven'. Also Celestia, Celestina, Celina   62

Celosia (Gk) 'flame'   49

Cerelia (Lat) 'of spring', the Roman goddess of sprouting corn and budding crops   49, 114

Ceridwen (Welsh) 'bright poetry'   60

Chandra (San) 'moonlike'   113

Charis (Gk) 'inspiring love', the root-word of 'charisma'   49, 73

Charity (Gk) 'love'. From the Greek *charitas*   57, 86

Charlene (OG) 'womanly'. A feminine form of Charles, derived recently from Charlotte. Also Charlena   39

Charlotta (OG) 'womanly'. Also Charlotte   38, 46, 47, 73

Charmian (Gk) 'drop of joy'. In Shakespeare's *Antony and Cleopatra*, Charmian is the faithful companion of the doomed Egyptian queen   73, 125

Chausiku (Swahili) 'born at night'   113

Chelsea (Eng) a place name   66

Chere (Fr) 'dear'. Cher is really a masculine form. Also Cherie, Cherry, Cheryl, Sher, Sherry   39, 40, 96, 115

Chiara (It) 'bright', Italian form of Clare   64

Chloe (Gk) 'green shoot', the springtime name for Demeter, goddess of Earth, as she brings forth blossom   38, 114

Chloris (Gk) 'blooming', the Greek goddess of flowers   47, 80, 114

Choomia (Gipsy) 'kiss'   59

Christabel (Gk/Lat) 'beautiful Christian'. A compound form found in mediaeval England   49

Christiane (Lat) 'Christian', via the Greek. Also Chrisoula, Christian, Christiana, Christiania, Christina, Christine, Kirsten, Kirstie, Krystian, Kristin, Kristina, Kristine, Kristyan   41, 47, 65, 76, 99

Christmas (Lat) 'born at Christmas', used for both sexes   117

Chryseis (Gk) 'daughter of the golden one'   49, 115

Chrysogon (Gk) 'golden-born'   115

Cicely (Lat) 'blind'   46

Claire (Lat) 'bright'   78

Clara (Lat) 'bright'. This is the word, a Latin adjective, from which Claire, Clare, and their derivatives have sprung. Clara, used in the Middle Ages, returned to popularity in the eighteenth century as part of the appetite for Latin-sounding names   43

Clare (Lat) 'bright'. A male name until St Clare of Assisi (1194–1253) founded her order, the Poor Clares, seizing the name for women   45, 78

Claribel (Lat) 'bright and beautiful'. The name appears in Shakespeare's *The Tempest* (1611)   96

Clarice (Lat) 'bright'. A French mediaeval form of Clare   49

Clarinda (Lat) A fanciful eighteenth-century form of Clare from the literary and latinising vogue   15, 114, 123

Clarissa (Lat) Latinised version of the French form of Clare, Clarice   47, 70, 73, 97

Claudette (Lat) 'lame'. From the Claudian clans of Rome, a French pet version   96

Claudia (Lat) 'lame', from the Claudian gens of Rome   4, 15, 70, 73

Cleantha (Gk) 'glorious flower'. Also Cliantha   115

Clementina (Lat) 'merciful'. Also Clementia, Clementine   49, 70, 85, 97, 99

Clematis (Lat) The name of a large-bloomed climbing plant   115

Cleopatra (Gk) 'her father's glory'. Name of the seductive charismatic and beautiful queen of Egypt with whom the ancient world's most powerful men, Mark Antony and Julius Caesar, both had passionate, desperate love affairs. Also Cleo, Cleta and Clio   41, 65, 95, 125

Clodagh (Irish) A river name, used as a personal name in the twentieth-century

Clodia (Lat) The name of a Roman beauty to whom Catullus addressed his love poems   4

Clorinda (Lat) 'renowned'. Coined as a name by the Italian poet Tasso

Clotilda (OG) 'battle-maiden'

Clover (Eng) 'to cling'. A white or purple blooming meadow-cover   55, 115

Clytie (Gk) 'splendid'. A nymph who died of love for the sun-god and took root to become the sun-loving heliotrope plant   115

Cody (OE) 'a cushion', used for both sexes   75, 99

Colette (Gk) 'victory of the people'. French pet version of the name Nicholas

Colleen (Irish) 'girl'   41, 96

Columbine (Lat) 'dove'. Harlequin's sweetheart in panto. Also Columba, Columbia, Columbina   80

Comfort (Lat) 'solace'. Given to both sexes by the Puritans   57

Conception (Lat) 'to begin'. Also Concepcion, Concha, Conchita   114

Concordia (Lat) 'harmony', the Roman goddess of peace after war

Constance (Lat) 'steadfast'. The name of yet another of William the Conqueror's daughters. Also Constancia, Constancy, Constanta, Constantia, Constantina, Constanza, Konstanze   43, 57, 70

Consuela (Lat) 'to cheer up'. A male name given a feminine ending, it is a Spanish Catholic name honouring Our Lady of Consolation   64

Cora (Gk) 'maiden', a name for spring-goddess Persephone. Also Corabel, Corabelle, Coralie, Corella, Coretta, Corie, Corinna, Corinne, Corita, Corrina, Kora   49, 78

Coral (Gk) 'pebble', but now meaning the hardened pinky-red secretion of seabed life forms used in making jewellery. Also Coralie and Coraline   49, 55, 95

Cordelia (Welsh) 'sea-jewel', or Latin 'warm-hearted'. One of the tragic princesses in Shakespeare's *King Lear*   97, 125

Corisande (OF) a name from mediaeval romance   49

Cornelia (Lat) feminine form of the Roman Cornelius clan 4, 49, 97

Cosima (Gk) 'universal harmony.' Also Kosima 65

Courtney (OF) 'short-nose'. An aristocratic surname now used as a first name by both sexes

Cressida (Gk) 'daughter of the golden one', the eponymous heroine of Shakespeare's *Troilus and Cressida* 73, 125

Crispina (Lat) 'curly-locks'. Female version of Crispin 49

Crystal (Gk) 'ice', now meaning 'diamond-like' 55, 96, 117

Cymry (Welsh) 'of Wales', for both sexes 60

Cynthia (Gk) 'of Mount Cynthos'. One of the names of Artemis or Diana, the Divine Huntress of Greek mythology, who was born there. Also a name used by poets to flatter Elizabeth I. Also Cindy, Cynthiana, Kynthia 78

Cyrilla (Gk) 'noble'. Feminine version of Cyril

D

Dagmar (Dan) 'joy of the Dane' 60, 63

Dahlia (Lat) The big-bloomed flower named botanically after the eighteenth-century Swede, Anders Dahl 56

Daisy (OE) 'day's-eye', a flower, and a nickname for Margaret, after St Margherita of Italy whose symbol was the simple daisy 43, 56, 96, 112

Dale (OE) 'valley', used for both sexes. Also Dayle 39, 41, 99

Damaris (Gk) 'calf-like'. Also Damara, Damita 49, 95

Dana (ON) 'from Denmark'. Also Dania 39

Danica (Sla) 'morning-star' 63, 112

Danielle (Heb) 'God has judged'. Female of Daniel 41

Danni (Heb) 'God has judged'; short version of Danielle and Daniella 39

Daphne (Gk) 'bay-tree'. Daphne was the Greek nymph loved by sun-god Apollo. She turned into a bush to evade his amorous advances   97

Daria (Pers) 'queenly'. Also Dari, Darice, Darya   89

Darlene (OE) 'darling'. Also Darleen, Darline, Daryl   39

Davina (Heb) 'friend'. A female Scots form of David. Also Davene, Davida, Davinia, Davita   15

Dawn (OE) 'daybreak'   39, 96, 112, 123

Deanna (Lat) 'divine'. A modern spelling of Diana which can be used as a feminine form of Dean. Also Deena   95

Deborah (Heb) 'bee'. Deborah was both a prophetess and a judge in the Bible. Also: Debbi, Debbie, Debby, Debera, Debra, Devorah   39, 41, 75, 97

Decima (Lat) 'tenth'   110

Dee (Welsh) 'dark'

Deirdre (Irish) 'sorrowful'. Also Diedra, Dierdra, Dierdre   60, 70, 98, 123

Delia (Gk) 'from Delos'. A name for the divine huntress Artemis, born on the island of Delos. Also Delinda, Della   98

Delicia (Lat) 'delight'. Also Delizia

Delilah (Heb) 'delight'. Gorgeous Delilah betrayed Samson to the Philistines   13, 49, 95

Delphina (Gk) 'dolphin'. Also Delfina, Delfine, Delphine, Delphinie   80

Delta (Gk) 'fourth'   110

Demetria (Gk) 'follower of Demeter'. Demeter was the Greek goddess of cultivation. She took a special interest in the harvest. Also Demeter, Demetra, Demetris, Dimitra   80

Denise (Gk) 'of Dionysus', a fertility god associated with wine and sexual rapture. The name is a female form of Denis. Also Denice, Denyse   12, 41

Deodata (Gk) 'god-given'

Desdemona (Gk) 'woman of ill fortune'. Shakespeare's

tragic heroine of that name is murdered by her jealous husband in *Othello* 125

Desiderata (Lat) 'longed-for'. Also Desiree 95, 119

Devon (OE) 'of Devon'. Also Devona, Devonna 66

Diamanta (Gk) 'adamantine, unconquerable' 55

Diamond (Gk) 'diamond' 55

Diana (Lat) 'divine'. The Roman version of Artemis, goddess of chastity, hunting and the moon. Also Deanna, Diane, Dianna, Dianora, Dionne, Dyane 41, 45, 73, 113

Diantha (Gk) 'flower of the gods' 80

Dido (Gk) 'teacher'. Dido, Queen of Carthage, killed herself when her Trojan lover Aeneas left Carthage to fulfil his own destiny 49, 129

Dieudonnee (Lat) 'gift-of-god', Frenchified 119

Dilys (Welsh) 'perfect' 49, 60

Dinah (Heb) 'vindicated' 41

Dionysia (Gk) 'follower of Dionysus', god of fertility, wine, and unblushing enjoyment of sex. Also Dionyza 49, 125

Divina (Lat) 'divine'. Also Diva 95

Dixie (ON) 'sprite'. Also 'tenth' 110

Dodie (Gk) 'gift', a diminutive of Dora 75

Dolores (Lat) 'sorrowful'. From Our Lady of Sorrows, Santa Maria de los Dolores

Domina (Lat) 'lady'

Dominica (Lat) 'of the Lord'. Also Domeniga, Domenica 47

Dominique (Lat) 'of the Lord', a French version 95, 111

Donata (Lat) 'given by God' 119

Donna (It) 'lady', a noun-turned-name 39, 96

Dora (Gk) 'gift'. Also Dolly 119

Dorabella (Gk) 'lovely gift', a compound form of Greek and Italian 127

Dorcas (Gk) 'gazelle'. Also Dorcia 54, 125, 129

Doreen (Gk) 'gift of God' 54, 123

Doria (Gk) 'from Doric regions' 95

Dorinda (Gk) 'gift of God'. A fanciful eighteenth-century version of Dorothy 123

Doris (Gk) 'gift'. Also Dorice, Dorita, Dorris, Dorrit 54

Dorothy (Gk) 'gift of God'. Also Dorothea 78, 98, 119, 129

Druella (OG) 'elf-vision' 49

Drusilla (Lat) Feminine form of Drusus, a name used by the Livian clan. One Drusilla was mistress of Caligula 4, 49

Dudee (Gipsy) 'star' 59

Dulcibella (Lat) 'sweet-beauty', a compound name. Also Dulcia, Dulciana, Dulcie, Dulcine, Dulcinea 96

E

Eartha (OE) 'of earth' 88

Easter (OE) 'Easter', a name given to both sexes 114

Ebony (Gk) 'ebony'. Also Ebonia 95

Edda (ON) 'poetry'. Also Eda 49

Edburga (OE) 'rich-fort' 8

Eden (OE) 'rich'. Or Hebrew, 'delight' 80

Edina (OE) 'rich friend'

Edith (OE) 'rich and war-lucky' 6, 17, 54, 70

Ediva (OE) 'rich gift' 119

Edna (Heb) 'rejuvenation' 54

Edwina (OE) 'rich friend'. A nineteenth-century form of Edwin 70

Eglentyne (OF) 'sweet-briar'. Also Eglantyne 17, 49, 56

Eileen (Irish) 'pleasant' 41, 98

Elaine (Gk) 'bright'. Old French form of Helen 17, 123

Eldora (Sp) 'golden' 80

Eleanor (Gk) 'bright'. Old French form of Helen. Also Eleanora, Elena, Eleni, Elinor, Lenora, Lenore, Leonora 9, 45, 98, 125

Electra (Gk) 'brilliant'. Also Elektra   49, 65, 80, 115

Elfreda (OE) 'elf-neat'   6, 49, 85

Elgiva (OE) 'elf-gift'   6

Elisheva (Heb) 'God is my satisfaction'   13

Elizabeth (Heb) 'God is my satisfaction'. Also Elisa, Elisabet, Elisabeta, Elisabeth, Elisabetta, Elise, Elissa, Eliza, Elizabet, Elize, Elsa, Elsebet, Elsie, Elspet, Elspeth, Elysa, Elyssa, Helsa, Isabel, Libby, Lilian, Lisa, Ysabel   12, 43, 45, 47, 98

Elizabella (Heb) 'God is my satisfaction'. This sixteenth-century form of Elizabeth was probably coined to flatter Queen Elizabeth. 'Bella' means 'beautiful' in Italian

Ella (OG) 'all', or Old English, 'elfin'   9, 17

Ellen (Gk) 'bright', diminutive of Helen   43, 127

Eloise (OG) 'flourishing'. Also Heloise and Helewise   49

Elsa (OG) 'noble'   47, 127

Elspeth (Heb) A Scots form of Elizabeth

Elysia (Gk) 'bliss'   47, 49, 95, 115

Emblem (Fr) 'emblem', a green jewel. Also Emmeline   55

Emerald (Fr) 'emerald', a green jewel   55, 115

Emily (Lat) from the Roman clan, Aemilius   38, 70, 98

Emma (OG) 'universal'. Name of the Norman queen of Ethelred the Unready   10, 17, 38, 45, 78

Emmeline (OG) 'industrious'   10, 49

Ena (Irish) 'little fiery one'. An English version of Eithne   60

Enid (Welsh) 'flawless'. Geraint's wife in Arthurian legend   17, 49, 54, 123

Erica (ON) 'ever-ruling'

Erin (Irish) 'peace'

Erma (OG) 'universal'. Also Irma   63, 89

Ermengarde (OE) 'guarded by the god Irmin'

Ernestine (OG) 'earnest'   49, 70

Esme (Lat) 'loved'. Also Amy

Esmeralda (Sp) 'emerald', a green jewel. Esme can be a short form   55, 124

Estelle (Lat) 'star'. Also Estella, Estrella, Estrellita, Stella   49, 64, 124

Esther (Heb) 'myrtle', or Persian 'star'   70

Estrild (OE) 'Easter-battle'   6, 49, 114

Ethel (OE) 'noble'   6, 7, 54

Ethelfleda (OE) 'noble-clan'   6

Euclea (Gk) 'glory'   115

Eugenia (Gk) 'well-born, of the best stock'. Also Eugenie   49, 64, 70, 73

Eulalia (Gk) 'sweet-talking'   49, 87

Eunice (Gk) 'happy victory'   49, 70

Eva (Heb) 'life-giving breath'. Also Evadne, Eve, Evie, Evita   63, 75, 78, 98

Evangeline (Gk) A name made up by the poet Long-fellow, from the Greek word for the Gospel   88, 124

Evelina (OF) 'hazel-tree'. Also Eveline   49, 62, 114

Evelyn (OF) 'hazel-tree', a name used for both sexes   99, 114

F

Fabia (Lat) 'bean-grower'. Of the Roman Fabius family. Also Fabiana and Fabiola

Faith (Lat) 'fidelity', one of the three great Christian virtues. Also Fae, Fay, Fidelity, Fidella   43, 57

Faline (Lat) 'cat-like'

Fallon (Irish) 'ruler's grandchild'   40

Fanchon (Lat) 'from France'

Farrah (Arab) 'happiness'

Fatima (Arab) 'daughter of the Prophet'. Fatima was his youngest daughter

Faustine (Lat) 'lucky'   49

Fawn (Eng) a baby deer   95

Fay (OF) 'fairy'   96

Felicia (Lat) 'happiness'. Also Felcia and Feliciana   49, 62

Felicity (Lat) 'happiness'. Also Felicite, Felis, Felise, Felisia, Felisse, Felita, Feliza   57, 78

Fenella (Irish) 'white shoulders', an English form   124

Fern (OE) 'fern'. Also Ferne   56, 116

Fernanda (OG) 'adventurer'

Finola (Irish) 'white shoulders'. Also Finella, Finnuala, Fionnuala, Nuala   47

Fiona (Irish) 'white'. A version of Finola created by writer William Sharp (1855–1905). Also Fionna and Fione   46, 78

Flavia (Lat) 'yellow'. From Rome's Flavian clan. Also Flaviana, Flavilla   4, 47, 49, 80

Fleur (Fr) 'flower'. Also Fflyr, Fleurette, Flore, Flower   56, 96, 115, 124

Flora (Lat) 'flower'. From Flora, Roman goddess of spring and blossoming plants. Her lover was the West Wind; her festival – April 28th – was called the Floralia. Also Fiora, Fiore, Florella, Floria, Florinda, Florie, Floris, Florrie   47, 56, 80, 96, 114, 127

Florence (Lat) 'blossoming' and the name of the Tuscan Renaissance city. Also Fiorella, Fiorenza, Firenze, Floren, Florencia, Florentia, Florenz, Floria, Florina, Florinda, Floryn, Flossie, Flo   54, 66, 95, 114

Floriane (Lat) 'flowering'

Fortunata (Lat) 'lucky'. Also Fortune   57

Frances (Lat) 'from France'. Also Fanny, Francesca, Francine, Francisca, Franciscka, Francoise, Franziske, Frasquita   43, 46, 47, 62, 64, 70, 73, 78, 98, 125, 127, 129

Freda (OG) 'peace'. Also Fredella

Fredegonde (OG) 'peace-war'   6, 49

Frederica (OG) 'peace-rule'. Also Farica, Federica, Feriga, Fredericka, Frederika, Frederique, Frerika, Friederike, Fritze, Frydryka   15, 73

Freya (ON) in Norse mythology, Freya was goddess of the night and of love. She was the sister of the god of fertility, Frey, and the daughter of Air and Water   49, 60, 80, 111

Friday (ON) 'Freya's day'   111

Frideswide (OE) 'peace-strong'   6, 111

Frieda (OG) 'peace'   78

Fronde (OE) 'frond'   49, 116

Frusannah (Lat/Heb) eighteenth and nineteenth-century compound name formed from Frances and Susannah   49

Fulvia (Lat) ambitious Roman woman whose third husband was Mark Antony. She appears in Shakespeare's *Antony and Cleopatra*   49, 80

G

Gabriel (Heb) 'strong of God'. Also Gabriella and Gabrielle, the Italian and French forms   64, 96

Gaea (Gk) 'Earth-mother'   88

Gaenor (Welsh) 'fair'. Also Gay, Gaynor

Gail (Heb) 'father's joy'. Also Gael, Gale, Gayle   41, 78

Galiena (OG) 'tall'   49, 95

Galina (Gk) 'calm'. A Russian form of Helena   62

Gardenia (Lat) A large, fragrant-bloomed shrub named in botanical dog-Latin after Alexander Garden (1730–91)   56

Garnet (Lat) 'pomegranate'. The red-seeded fruit lent its name to the crimson jewels called garnets   55, 116

Gemma (Lat) 'gem'   46, 78

Genevia (Lat) 'juniper'. Also Geneva, Genevra, Genna, Ginevra   49, 66

Genista (Lat) 'broom-flower'   116

Genevieve (OG) 'womankind'. St Genevieve is a patron saint of Paris   96

Georgette (Gk) 'farmer'. Georgette is a version of George. Also Georgia, Georgiana, Georgina 38, 47, 66, 88, 95, 96, 99

Geraldine (OG) a name made up by the sixteenth-century romantic poet the Earl of Surrey to conceal the identity of Lady Elizabeth Fitzgerald, to whom he wrote love poems 78, 99, 124

Gerda (ON) In Norse myth, Gerda was the wife of Frey and the daughter of the frost giant

Germaine (Lat) 'a German' 80

Gertrude (OG) 'spear-strong' Gertrude was one of the twelve Valkyries, and the name of Hamlet's mother in Shakespeare's *Hamlet*. Also Gartrude, Gertradine, Gertraud, Gertruda, Gertrudis 6, 54, 70, 89, 125

Gervasia (OG) 'spear'

Ghislaine (OG) 'pledge' 49

Gilda (OE) 'golden' 49, 116, 127

Gillian (Lat) a form of Julius, the Roman family name 46, 96

Gina (Lat) 'queen'. A short form of Regina 78

Giralda (OG) 'spear-rule'. Italian feminine version of Gerald

Gisela (OG) 'pledge'. Also Gisèle, Giselle 10, 80, 95

Gladys (Welsh) 'princess' or Welsh vestige of Claudius, a Roman name meaning 'lame' 54

Glenda (Eng) feminised form of the surname-turned-name Glenn. Also Glenna 41, 49, 70, 88

Gloria (Lat) 'glory'. Also Gloriane, Glory 41, 95

Gloriana (Lat) a name used to flatter Elizabeth I 95

Glynis (Welsh) 'glen'. Also Glenna, Glennis, Glenys, Glynnis, Glynwen 41, 60

Godiva (OE) 'God's gift'. Also Godeva, Godgifu 6, 49, 95

Golda (OE) 'gold'. Also Goldarina, Goldia, Goldie, Goldina 55, 116

Grace (Lat) 'grace'. Gracia, Grata, Gratia, Gratiana, Grazia, Graziella, Grazina 43, 57, 70

Gracilia (Lat) 'slender'   49

Grainne (Irish) 'love'. Also Grania   49

Greer (Gk) 'watchman'

Gregoria (Gk) 'watchman'

Greta (Eng) 'daisy'. The German and Scandinavian short form of Margaret, now a name in its own right. Also Greda, Gretchen, Grete, Gretel   63, 64

Griselda (OG) 'grey battlemaid'. The patient heroine of Chaucer's *The Clerk's Tale*, borrowed from Boccaccio. Also Grisel, Griseldis, Grisell, Grisilda, Grissel, Grissil, Grizel, Grizelda, Grizzel   80, 85

Gudrun (ON) 'rune'

Guinevere (Welsh) 'fair'. King Arthur's queen, who betrayed her husband with Sir Lancelot. Also Guener, Guenever, Guenevere, Guenna, Gunnora, Jenifer, Jennifer, Vanora   6, 49, 60, 80

Gunhilda (ON) 'battle-strife'. Also Gunilda, Gunnilla   6, 89

Gussie (Lat) 'venerable'. A short form of Augusta. Also Gussy   43

Gwawl (Welsh) 'light'

Gwawr (Welsh) 'dawn'   60

Gwendolyn (Welsh) 'white moon'. Also Guendolen, Gwen, Gwendoline, Gwendolen   49, 78, 98

Gwyneth (Welsh) 'white maiden'. Also Gwyn, Gwynaeth, Gwynedd, Gynedd   60

H

Hadassah (Heb) 'myrtle'   13

Haidee (Gk) 'caress'   50, 75, 96

Halcyone (Gk) 'kingfisher'   50, 115

Hannah (Heb) 'graceful'. Also Hana, Hanna, Hanne, Hanni, Hannie, Anna, Anne, Nancy   38, 43, 63, 70, 78

Harriet (OG) 'home-ruler'. Also Harrietta, Harriette, Hetty 43, 70, 78, 98

Hayley (OE) 'hay-meadow', a surname-turned-name

Hazel (Eng) 'hazel tree' 56, 96, 114

Heather (Eng) 'heather' 56, 96, 116

Hebe (Gk) 'youth'. Zeus's daughter, the Greek goddess of youth 50, 112, 114

Hedda (OG) 'struggle'

Heidi (OG) 'nobility'. Also Adalheid 64, 75

Helen (Gk) 'bright'. Also Elena, Eleni, Ellene, Ellie, Ellyn, Helena, Helene, Yelena 9, 43, 62, 64, 65, 70, 75, 78, 98, 113, 125

Helga (ON) 'pious'

Hella (ON) 'bright' 47

Heloise (OG) 'flourishing' 10

Henrietta (OG) 'mistress of the home'. Also Enrichetta, Enriqueta, Etta, Henriette, Hetty 46, 70, 73, 99

Hermia (Gk) feminine form of Hermes, messenger of the gods. Shakespeare used it in *A Midsummer Night's Dream* 80, 125

Hermione (Gk) A female version of Hermes, Greek messenger of the gods 80

Hero (Gk) 'chosen one'. In mythology, the priestess of Venus, goddess of love 125

Hesper (Gk) 'evening star' 117

Hester (Pers) 'myrtle' or 'star' 70

Hestia (Gk) Greek goddess of the hearth and home

Hieronyma (Heb) 'God is high'. Feminine form of Jerome

Hilary (Gk) 'cheerful', given to both sexes 99

Hilda (OG) 'battle'. Also Hild, Hilde, Hildy 6, 54, 63

Hildegard (OG) 'war-knowledge' 8

Hippolyta (Gk) 'free horse'. Hippolyta was queen of the Amazons, a race of tall, strong warrior women. Her father was the god of war 125

Holland (Eng) One of many place names currently fashionable as ambisexual first names 66

Holly (OE) 'holly'   56, 75, 98, 117

Honey (Eng) 'honey'

Honoria (Lat) 'honour'. Also Honor, Honora, Honour
50, 57

Hope (OE) 'hope'. One of the three chief Christian
virtues   43, 57, 86

Horatia (Lat) From the Horatii, a noble Roman clan
meaning 'of the hour'   50, 86, 88

Hortensia (Lat) 'garden'. Also Hortense and Ortensia   50

Hyacinth (Gk) 'hyacinth flower' and 'sapphire'. Also
Giacinta, Hyacintha, Hyacinthe, Jacenta, Jacinda,
Jacinta, Jacintha, Jacinthe   56, 96, 114

I

Ianthe (Gk) 'violet-flower'. In mythology, Ianthe was a
sea-nymph. The poet Shelley named his daughter
Ianthe in 1813. Also Iantha   114

Ida (OG) 'hard-working'   10

Idonea (ON) 'of Idhuna', the goddess of spring   114

Idris (Welsh) 'fiery one', common to both sexes   60

Ignatia (Lat) 'fiery'. Feminine version of Ignatius. Also
Ignacia   50

Ileana (Gk) 'a Trojan'; Ilium was the name of Troy   50

Ilka (Slav) 'beautiful'. Also Ilona and Ilonka   60, 63

Imelda (OE) 'moderate'

Imogen (Lat) 'image'. Also Imagina, Imogene   73, 98,
124, 125

India (San) 'river Indus'   66

Inge (ON) Ing was a Norse fertility god   60

Ingrid (ON) 'beloved of Ing'   6, 63, 98

Iola (Gk) 'dawn-cloud'   80, 114

Iolanthe (Gk) 'violet-flower'. Also Yolanda, Yolande

Iona (Gk) 'purple stone' or Scottish island of the same
name   55, 60

Iphigenia (Gk) princess sacrificed by her father King Agamemnon to bring luck before he and the Greeks sailed to rescue Helen from Troy 80

Irene (Gk) 'peace'. Also Irina 54, 62, 70

Iris (Gk) 'rainbow'. Iris, bridging heaven and earth, was the messenger of the Greek gods 56, 114, 125

Irma (OG) 'of Irmin', the god of war 54

Isabel (Heb) 'God is my satisfaction'. Variant of Elizabeth common in Scotland. Also Belicia, Isla, and Isobel 12, 98, 125

Isabella (Heb) 'God is my satisfaction'. Italian form of Elizabeth 64, 96, 125

Isadora (Gk) 'gift of Isis'. Isis was the Egyptian god of the moon and fertility 50, 80, 95

Isis (Egyptian) 'supreme goddess'. The queen of the gods in Egypt, ruler of the moon, fertility and motherhood 50, 95

Ismenia (Gk) 'learned'. Also Ismay, Ismena, Ismene 50

Isolda (OG) 'ice-rule'. Also Iseult and Isolde 80

Ivory (Lat) 'ivory' 95

Ivy (OE) 'ivy'. Also Iva 56, 117

J

Jacintha (Gk) 'hyacinth flower', 'hyacinth jewel'. Also Giacinta, Jacinda, Jacinta, Jacinth, Jacinthe, Jacynth, Jassinta 50, 55, 114

Jacobina (Heb) 'supplanter'. Also Jacoba 50

Jacqueline (Heb) 'supplanter'. Also Jaclyn, Jacquelyn 98

Jacquetta (Heb) 'supplanter'. Also Jacquenetta, Jacquette, Jaquetta 96, 125

Jade (Fr) 'jadite' or 'nephrite', the green and blue translucent gem stones. Also Ijada 41, 55

Jaime (Heb) 'supplanter'. A female form of James, which doubles as the French 'I love'

Jamesina (Heb) 'supplanter'. From James. Also Jamie 75

Jane (Heb) 'Jehovah has favoured'. From John. Also Hanna, Hanne, Jana – a modern Latinised form – and Jayne 41, 45, 130

Janet (Heb) 'Jehovah has favoured'. Scots version of Jane, derived from the French Jeanette. Also Jenella, Janetta, Janette, Jenetta, Jenette 41, 78

Janice (Heb) 'Jehovah has favoured'. A North American invention, derived from Jane. Also Janis 41, 99

Janine (Heb) 'Jehovah has favoured'. Also Jan, Janina, Janna 41, 62, 78, 98

Japonia (Lat) 'Japan'. Also Japonica, a Japanese quince plant

Jardena (Heb) 'flowing down'. Also Jordan, used for both sexes

Jasmine (Pers) 'jasmine blossom'. Also Gelsomina, Jasmin, Jasmina, Jessamine, Jessamy, Jessamyn, Yasmin, Yasmina, Yasmine 56

Jean (Heb) 'Jehovah has favoured'. Scots form of Joan, from the old French feminine of John, Jehane. Also Jeanette, Jeanne, Jeannette, Jehane 41, 64, 78, 96

Jemima (Heb) 'dove'. One of the daughters of Biblical Job. Also Jamima, Jemimah, Yemima

Jenna (Arab) 'little bird'. Also Jena 98

Jennifer (Welsh) 'fair' English form of Gwenhywvar, the Guinevere of Arthurian legend. Also Jenefer, Jenifer, Jenny, Jenufa 98, 127, 130

Jessica (Heb) 'God witnesses'. In *The Merchant of Venice*, Shakespeare calls Shylock's daughter by the name. Also Gessica, Jesca, Jessalin 38, 73, 98, 125

Jethra (Heb) 'excellent'. Feminine form of Jethro

Jetta (Gk) 'jet', the shiny black stone

Jewel (OF) 'gem'. Also Jewell, Jewelle 55

Jezebel (Heb) 'unesteemed, impure'. Also Jessabell, Jezabel, Jezabella, Jezabelle 95

Jill (Lat) 'downy'. A pet version of Gillian, a name

derived from the Julian clan of ancient Rome. Also Gill, Gillet, Gillian, Giula, Giuletta, Jillian 78

Joan (Heb) 'Jehovah has favoured'. Mediaeval English feminine of John, ousted in Tudor times by the name Jane. Also Joanna, Joanne, Joeann, Johan, Johanna, Johanne, Johna, Juana, Juanita, Siobhan, Zaneta 41, 45, 62, 70, 78, 98, 125, 130

Jocasta (Gk) 'shining moon' 47, 80

Jocelyn (OG) 'Gothic'. Used for both sexes. Also Jesseline, Jesslyn, Jocelin, Joceline, Jocelynde, Jocelyne, Joscelin, Joscelind, Josceline, Joscelyn, Josette, Josa, Josie, Joslyn, Joss, Josselin

Jodie (Heb) 'from Judah'. Also Jodi and Jody 75

Joelle (Heb) 'Jehovah is God'. Also Joel, Joella and Joellen

Jolie (Fr) 'pretty', an adjective turned name

Jonquil (Lat) 'jonquil', a narcissus-type flower with leaves like rushes. Also Jonquelle, Jonquille 56

Josephine (Heb) 'may Jehovah increase'. A French diminutive of the feminine of Joseph. Also Giuseppa, Giuseppina, Josee, Josefa, Josefina, Josefine, Josepha, Josephe, Josetta, Josette, Josie, Josy, Pepita, Peppina, Yosepha, Yosifa 70, 75, 96, 99, 117

Jovita (Lat) 'jolly', or 'born under Jupiter' 50

Joy (Lat) 'joy'. Also Gioia, Joia, Joya, Joye 57, 96

Joyce (Lat) 'merry'. Also Jocea, Jocosa, Joice, Joisse, Joss, Josse 41, 70, 78

Judith (Heb) 'of Judah'. Also Jude, Judi, Judie, Judy 41, 70, 75, 96

Julia (Lat) 'downy'. Feminine of Julius clan. Also Giulia, Giuliana, Juliana, Juliane, Julianne, Julie, Julienne, Julinda 4, 8, 46, 125

Juliet (Lat) 'little Julia'. Shakespeare's *Romeo and Juliet* seems to have introduced the name to England, in a translation of the Italian Giulietta. Also Juliette, Juliot, Julitta 8, 47, 78, 98, 127

June (Lat) 'of the sixth month, Junius' 115

Juno (Lat) Roman goddess of women and childbirth. Also an Old Irish variation of Oonagh, perhaps meaning 'lamb'

Justine (Lat) 'just'. Feminine version of Justin. Also Giustin, Justina and Justinia   4, 47, 50

K

Kali (San) 'energy'

Kalliope (Gk) 'beautiful'   65

Kara (ON) The Valkyrie who followed her hero to war in the form of a gracious singing swan. Also considered a diminutive form of Katharine   60

Karen (Dan) Danish form of Katharine. The name has enjoyed a long vogue in Britain, perhaps thanks to the 'Garth' strip cartoon character of that name in the *Daily Mirror*. Also Caren, Carin, Caryn, Kari, Karin, Karina, Karima, Karna, Karon, Karyn, Kerrin   40, 43, 63, 95

Karis (Gk) a rare beautiful·name, possibly from the Greek *charis*, meaning 'grace', or Latin *caritas*, 'charity'

Karolina (Lat) A feminine form of Charles   62

Kasamira (Slav) 'peacemaker'

Kassia (Gk) 'pure'   62

Katharine (Gk) 'pure'. Also Caitlin, Caitrin, Catarina, Caterina, Catherina, Catherine, Catriona, Caty, Ekaterina, Kata, Kate, Katerina, Katharina, Kathryn, Katie, Katina, Katja, Katrina, Katrinka, Katya, Katy, Kay, Kittie, Kitty   12, 41, 45, 62, 63, 64, 65, 70, 75, 78, 96, 99, 125

Kathleen (Irish) 'pure'. Irish diminutive of Katherine   98

Keely (Irish) 'beautiful'. Also Keeley, Keelia   60

Kefira (Heb) 'young lioness'

Kelda (ON) 'spring', fount of life   114

Kelly (Gk) 'woman of the Celtic warrior race'   40, 75

Kenna (OE) 'knowing, competent woman'

Kerry (Irish) 'dark-haired', 'from the dark race of Kerry' 75

Kezia (Heb) 'cinnamon'. One of Job's daughters. Also Keziah

Kim (OE) 'royal' 40, 99

Kimberley (OE) 'from the royal meadow' 41

Kira (Pers) 'sun'. Feminine form of Cyrus. Also Kiri 62, 75

Kirby (OE) 'from the church-town' 99

Kirsten (Lat) 'Christian'. Scandinavian form of Christine

Kirsty (Lat) 'Christian'. Pet Scottish form of Christine. Also Kirstie 41, 75, 96

Kora (Gk) 'maiden'. Kora was the daughter of Demeter, goddess of agriculture. Also Cora, Corabelle, Corella, Coretta, Corey, Corina, Corinna, Corinne, Coriss, Korella, Koren, Koressa, Korie

Kristen (Lat) 'Christian'. Scandinavian form of the English Christine. Also Krista, Kristan, Kristel, Kristi, Kristin, Kristina, Kristyn, Krysta, Krystyna

Krystle (Lat) Fanciful form of 'crystal'. Also Crystal 40, 117

Kylie (Australian) 'boomerang' 40

L

Lacey (Gk) 'cheerful'. Pet form of Larissa

Laetitia (Lat) 'joy'. Also Lecia, Leda, Leticia, Letitia, Letizia, Lettice, Tish 15

Lalage (Gk) 'babbler'. Also Lala, Lallie 115

Lana (Gk) 'light'. A form of Helen

Lara (Gk) 'cheerful'. Russian diminutive of Larissa 95

Larissa (Gk) 'cheerful'. Also Laryssa, Lissa 62, 95

Lark (Eng) 'singing bird' 112, 115

Laura (Lat) 'bay-tree', or 'from Laurentium'. Also Laure,

Laureen, Laurel, Lauren, Laurencia, Lauretta,
Laurette, Laurie, Laurine, Lora, Loreen, Lorene,
Lorenza, Loretta, Lorette, Lori, Lorrie   38, 41, 46, 47,
56, 64, 75, 98, 117

Lavender (Eng) 'lavender-flower'   56, 115

Laverne (OF) 'alder-tree' or 'of the spring'   114

Lavinia (Lat) 'purified'   15, 50, 73, 125

Leaf (Eng) 'leaf'   116

Leah (Heb) 'heifer' or 'weary'. Jacob's first wife. Also
Lia   64

Leandra (Lat) 'like a lioness'. Also Leodora, Leoine,
Leoline, Leonanie, Leonelle

Leda (Gk) 'lady'. Also Leta, Lida   50

Lee (OE) 'from the meadow'. Also Leigh

Leila (Pers) 'night'. Also Layla, Leilah, Leyla   95, 117

Lena (Gk) 'light', or Hebrew 'Magdalenian woman'

Lenore (Gk) 'light'. A Russian–German form of Eleanor.
Also Leonora   80, 113, 127

Leonarda (OG) 'bold'. Italian feminine of Leonard

Leonie (Gk) 'lion'. Also Leontina, Leontine, Leontyna
95

Leonora (Gk) 'light'. Also Leola, Leona, Leone, Leora
80

Lesley (Scot) 'from the garden by the pool'   99

Levanna (Lat) 'sun rising'   112

Lilac (Pers) 'lilac flower'   56, 115

Lilith (Arab) 'of the night'. Associated with lily-flower
118

Lillian (Heb) 'God is my satisfaction'. Also Lilian,
Liliane, Lilias, Lilike, Lilliana   43, 62, 63, 80, 98

Lily (Gk) 'lily-flower'   43, 56, 115

Linda (OG) 'serpent'   41, 98

Lindsay (OE) 'from the isle of linden trees'   41, 99

Linet (Fr) French form of Eluned, now with the associa-
tion of the little songbird, the linnet. Also Linette,
Linnet, Linnett, Lynnet, Lynette   50

Linnea (Lat) 'lime-tree blossom' and Sweden's blue national flower, named after Carolus Linnaeus (1707–78), who first produced a classification system for flora and fauna. Also Linnea 115

Lisa (Heb) 'God is my satisfaction'. Also Lise, Lisette, Liza 38, 41, 98

Livia (Lat) of the Roman Livian family. Also Liv 4, 47, 63

Lois (OG) 'glorious battle'. A form of Louise 41

Lola (Span) 'sorrowful'. A familiar of Dolores. Also Lolita 95

Lorna (Eng) a name invented by R. D. Blackmoor for the 1869 novel *Lorna Doone*. Romantic, windswept image 124

Lorraine (Fr) 'of Lorraine' 40, 98

Lotus (Gk) 'lotus flower'. Also Lotos 95

Louella (OG) a compound of Louise and Ella. Also Luella 87

Louisa (OG) 'glorious battle'. Also Luisa, Luiza 15, 47, 64, 98

Louise (OG) 'glorious battle'. Also Lulu 40, 46, 78

Loveday (Eng) 'born on loveday'. A loveday was an annual feast reserved for resolving disputes within mediaeval communities 50, 95

Lucasta (Lat) 'light'. Seventeenth-century form of Lucy 50, 80, 113, 124

Lucia (Lat) 'light'. Also Luce, Lucetta, Lucette, Luciana, Lucienne, Lucilla, Lucille, Lucina, Lucy 4, 47, 50, 64, 80, 125

Lucinda (Lat) 'light'. Seventeenth-century form of Lucy. Also Cindy 73, 124

Lucretia (Lat) of the Lucretian gens. Also Lucrece, Lucrecia, Lucresse, Lucrezia 4, 47, 95

Lucy (Lat) 'light' 46, 75

Ludmilla (Slav) 'beloved of the people' 62

Lundy (Welsh) 'idol'. Now associated, via French, with Monday 111

Lydia (Gk) 'from Lydia', the kingdom in Asia Minor of
   rich King Croesus   95
Lynn (Welsh) 'idol', From Eluned. Also Lyn, Lynette
   78, 96
Lyris (Gk) 'lyre'   50
Lysandra (Gk) 'free'

M

Mabel (Lat) 'lovable'. Also Amabel, Amabella, Mab,
   Mabella, Mabelle, Mabilla. Mab was queen of the
   fairies and is associated with powers of bewitch-
   ment   17, 43, 50, 54
Madeline (Heb) 'woman of Magdala'. Also Maddelena,
   Medeline, Magda, Magdalena, Magdalene, Malena,
   Malina, Lena, Lene   12, 46, 98
Madonna (It) 'my lady'. The name given to the Virgin as
   the Mother of Christ   95
Madra (Lat) 'mother', a Spanish name. Also Madre
Maeve (Irish) from Maedbh, the third-century queen of
   Connacht   60
Magnolia (Lat) 'magnolia blossom', named botanically
   for Pierre Magnol   56, 115
Maia (Gk) the blonde daughter of Atlas and mother of
   Hermes. In Roman myth, she was seen as the Earth
   mother and her feast was celebrated on 1 May   80
Mairead (OF) 'judge', an Irish name   60
Mairin (Heb) 'wished-for child'. Irish form of Mary, and
   a diminutive of Maire   60
Maisie (Fr) 'daisy'. A pet form of Margaret   43, 97
Mallory (Fr) 'armoured one'. Also Mallorie, Malorie,
   Malory
Malvina (Scot) 'polished'   50
Mamie (Fr) 'daisy'. Diminutive of Margaret
Manuela (Heb) 'God is with us'

Mara 'wished-for child'. Also Marah   50

Marcella (Lat) 'little Marcus', of Mars the god of war. Also Marcelle, Marcellina, Marcelline   50, 127

Marcia (Lat) 'of Mars'. Also Marcie, Marcy, Marsha   75

Margaret (Fr) 'daisy'. Also Daisy, Greta, Gretal, Gretchen, Gretel, Madge, Mae, Maergrethe, Maggie, Maidie, Maisie, Mamie, Margareta, Margarethe, Margarida, Margarita, Margaux, Marghanita, Margherita, Marguerita, Marguerite, Meg, Mergret, Peg, Peggy, Rita   43, 45, 63, 64, 75, 78, 87, 95

Margery (Fr) 'daisy'. Also Marjorie   78, 98, 125

Margot (Fr) 'daisy'. Also Margaux, Margo   78, 80, 98

Maria (Heb) 'wished-for child'   97, 130

Marian (Heb) 'wished-for child'. Also Mariana, Marianne, Marion   78, 125, 127

Maribel (Eng) 'pretty Mary', a compound name deriving from Hebrew and French

Marie (Heb) 'wished-for child'. Also Marietta, Mariette   64, 78, 95

Mariel (Heb) 'wished-for child'. A Dutch form of Mary

Marigold (Eng) compound of 'Mary' and 'gold', also the name of a sun-loving orange flower   56, 97, 115

Marilyn (Eng) compound of Maria and Lyn. Also Marlene   40, 41

Marina (Lat) 'of the sea'. Also Marine, Marinna, Maris, Marissa, Marnie, Marris, Meris   62, 64, 95, 125, 127

Mariposa (Sp) 'butterfly'   115

Marlene (Eng) contraction of Maria-Magdalene, invented by Marlene Dietrich from her own name   42

Martha (Aram) 'lady'. Also Marta, Marte   62, 70

Martina (Lat) 'of Mars', god of war. Also Martine, Tina   41, 98

Mary (Heb) 'wished-for child'. Also Marice, Mariquilla, Marquita, Maris, Marisa, Marisol, Mariska, Marita, Maritsa, Maryse, Mascha, Masha, Maura, Maure,

Maurita, May, Meriel, Meryl, Mitzi, Molly   12, 45, 64, 75, 96, 114, 118, 131

Matilda (OG) 'battle-strong'. Also Mathilda, Mathilde, Matilde, Matilldis, Matya, Metilda, Tilda   10, 17, 43, 70

Maud (OG) 'battle-strong'. A form of Matilda. Also Maude   10, 17, 43, 54, 80

Maureen (Heb) 'wished-for child'. Irish form of Mary. Also Marie, Maura   60, 99

Mavis (Fr) 'songthrush'   50, 115, 124

Maxine (Lat) 'little greatest'. Also Maxima, Maxime, Maxi, Maxie   40, 41

May (Lat) 'of Maia', the fertility deity whose festival occurred on May Day. Now means simply 'of May'. Also Mae   114, 130

Medea (Gk) Bewitching temptress of ancient Greece   50, 110

Megan (Fr) 'daisy'. Familiar Welsh form of Margaret   41, 60, 98

Melanie (Gk) 'dark one'. Also Melania   41, 97, 118

Melantha (Gk) 'dark flower'   50, 95, 118

Melina (Gk) 'song'   50, 80

Melinda 'dark'   50, 80

Melissa (Gk) 'honeybee' or 'lemon balm'. Also Melisa, Melita, Melitta   41, 95, 115

Melody (Gk) 'song'   40, 96

Melora (Gk) 'golden fruit'   50

Melosa (Sp) 'honey-sweet'

Meraud (Cornish) 'of the sea'. An old Cornish name, rare outside the Duchy   60

Mercedes (Sp) 'mercies'

Mercia (OE) 'of Mercia'   50

Mercy (Lat) 'compassion'

Meriel (Irish) 'bright sea'. An older, prettier form of Muriel   50, 80

Merle (Fr) 'blackbird'   115

Merry (Lat) 'compassion'. A pet-name of Mercy, also now associated with the adjective 'merry' 75, 96

Meryl (Heb) 'wished-for child'. A variant of Mary

Meta (Lat) 'ambition achieved' 111

Mia (It) 'mine' 95

Michaela (Heb) 'like the Lord'. Also Micaela, Miguella, Mikelina, Mimi 73, 127

Michele (Heb) 'like the Lord'. Also Michal, Michel, Michelle

Mildred (OE) 'gentle strength'. Also Meldred, Mildrid 8, 54

Milena (OG) 'gentle'

Millicent (OG) 'work-strong'. Also Melicent, Melisande, Melisenda, Melisendra, Mellicent, Mellisent, Millie, Milly 43, 75

Mina (Lat) 'threat' 64

Minerva (Lat) goddess of wisdom 80

Mira (Lat) 'marvellous'. Also Mirabel, Myra 54, 97, 124

Miri (Gipsy) 'my own' 59

Miranda (Lat) 'astonishing'. Probably invented by Shakespeare for *The Tempest*, his magical island play 47, 73, 80, 95, 125

Miriam (Heb) 'wished-for child'. Miriam – or Mrym as it was originally – is the pure root of the name Mary and all the amalgams it has accreted over the centuries

Modesty (Lat) 'modesty'. Also Modesta, Modestia, Modestine 57

Moira (Heb) 'wished-for child'. An Irish form of Mary, or Maire. Also the name for the three Greek Fates who controlled human life 41, 60, 70

Mona (Gk) 'alone', Arabic 'hope', or Irish 'little noble'

Monica (Lat) 'adviser'. Also Monika, Monique 41, 64, 70, 97, 98

Morag (Scot) 'sun' 54, 70

Morgana (Welsh) 'verge of the sea' 50, 80

Morna (Irish) 'beloved' 60

Morwenna 'sea-wave' 50, 60

Muriel (Irish) 'bright-sea'. Also Merril, Merrill, Merryl, Murial 54

Musette (OF) 'thought' 50

Myfanwy (Welsh) 'my precious treasure'. Also Fanny 60

Myrna (Arab) 'myrrh'. Merna, Mirna

Myrtle (Gk) 'myrtle', the perfumed evergreen shrub of Venus 56

N

Nadia (Slav) 'hope' 50, 70

Nadine (Slav) 'hope'. From the Russian, via French 98

Nancy (Heb) 'graceful' 41, 97, 131

Nanette (Heb) 'graceful' 41, 97

Naomi (Heb) 'delightful'. Also Naoma 98

Nara (OE) 'near, dear one' 50, 60

Natalia (Lat) 'Christmas-born'. Also Natalie, Natalya 62, 70, 98, 118

Natasha (Lat) 'Christmas-born'. Diminutive of Natalia 118

Nebula (Lat) 'misty' 118

Neda (Slav) 'Sunday-born' 111

Nellwyn (OE) 'Eleanor's friend' 50

Neoma (Gk) 'new moon' 114

Nerissa (Gk) 'sea-nymph'. Also Nerina, Nerine, Nerita 95, 125

Nerys (Welsh) 'lady' 97

Nicola (Gk) 'victory of the people'. Also Nichola, Nichole, Nicole, Nicolette 41, 46, 78, 97, 118

Nina (Heb) 'graceful', or Spanish 'little girl' 98

Nissa (Heb) 'sign' 50, 118

Noelle (OF) 'Christmas-born' 118

Nona (Lat) 'ninth' 110

Nora (Lat) 'honour'. A short Irish form of Honoria   60, 71
Noreen (Lat) 'honour'. Irish diminutive of Honoria   41
Norma (Lat) 'model'   41, 71, 127
Norna (ON) the Fates of Norse mythology   44
Nuala (Irish) 'white-shouldered'. From Fionnuala   60
Nydia (Gk) 'fledgling'   69
Nyssa (Gk) 'beginning'   80

O

Octavia (Lat) 'eighth'   110, 125
Odelia (Gk) 'song'   50
Odessa (Gk) 'wanderings'   66, 95
Odette (OG) 'fatherland's inheritor'   47
Ola (ON) 'nourisher'   60
Olga (ON) 'holy'. A popular Russian name today   62, 127
Olive (Lat) 'olive-tree'   54
Olivia (Lat) 'olive-tree'   38, 73, 98, 125
Olwyn (Welsh) 'white footprint'   60
Olympia (Gk) 'heavenly'   65, 95, 127
Oonagh (Irish) 'lamb'. Also Oona, Una   54
Opal (San) 'gem'   55
Ophelia (Gk) 'aid'   80, 125
Ora (Lat) 'prayer'   115
Oralia (Lat) 'golden' Also Oralie   50, 80
Oriana (Lat) 'dawn'. Also Oria, Oriande, Oriane   50, 65, 95, 115
Oriel (Lat) 'golden'. Also Oriole   10, 50
Ortrud (OG) 'golden maid'   127

P

Pallas (Gk) 'wise', from Pallas Athene, goddess of wisdom   50, 65

Paloma (Lat) 'dove' 80

Pamela (Gk) 'all-honey', a made-up literary name 97, 115

Pamina (Arab) 'daughter of the Queen of the night' 113, 118

Pandora (Gk) 'wholly gifted' 73, 95

Pansy (Fr) 'to think', and flowers of the viola species 56, 97, 115

Panthea (Gk) 'of all the gods', all-blessed 50

Paris (Fr) French capital 66

Pascale (Lat) 'Easter-born'. Also Pascal, Pascaline, Pascha, Paschal, Pashell, Pasqua 114

Patience (Lat) 'to endure'. Also Patia 57, 125

Patrice (Lat) 'noble' 99

Patricia (Lat) 'noble'. Also Pat, Patsy, Patti 73, 75, 98

Paula (Lat) 'small'. Also Paola, Paolina, Paulita 41, 71, 78, 98

Pauline (Lat) 'small'. Also Pauletta, Paulette, Paulina 41, 78, 97, 98

Pearl (Eng) 'pearl' 55

Peggy (Fr) 'daisy'. Also Peg, Pegeen 75

Penelope (Gk) 'weaver'. Pelcha, Peneli, Penelopa, Penny 70, 75, 98

Penthea (Gk) 'the fifth' 110

Perdita (Lat) 'the lost'. Invented by Shakespeare for *The Winter's Tale* 124, 125

Pernella (Gk) 'rock'. Also Pernelle 50

Persephone (Gk) A goddess of spring 50, 80, 118

Persis (Gk) 'woman of Persia'. Also Persia 50, 66

Petra (Gk) 'stone'. Also Perrine, Peta, Piera, Petrina, Petronella, Petronia, Petronille, Pierina, Pietra 4, 50, 55, 64, 73, 80, 118

Phaedra (Gk) 'bright'. Also Phedra, Phedre 50, 80, 113

Phebe (Gk) 'shining'. Also Phoebe 115, 125

Phemie (Gk) 'of good repute', a diminutive of Euphemia 80

Philana (Gk) 'people-lover'. Also Philene, Philina 50
Philantha (Gk) 'flower-lover' 115
Philippa (Gk) 'horse-lover'. Also Pip, Pippa 75, 98
Philomena (Gk) 'lover of song' 73, 115
Phyllida (Gk) 'leafy' 73, 98, 114
Phyllis (Gk) 'leafy' 73, 114
Pilar (Sp) 'column', a name for the Virgin Mary 65
Placida (Lat) 'calm'. Also Placidia 50
Pleasance (OF) 'delightful' 95
Polly (Heb) 'wished-for', diminutive of Mary 43, 75, 98
Pomona (Lat) 'fruit' 50, 116
Poppy (Lat) 'poppy' 56, 75, 115
Portia (Lat) 'pig' 80, 125
Posy (Eng) 'nosegay of flowers' 56, 115
Prima (Lat) 'first' 97, 109
Primavera (Lat) 'first-of-spring' 114
Primrose (Lat) 'first rose' 56, 114
Priscilla (Lat) 'pristine' 4, 70
Prospera (Lat) 'prosperous' 50
Prudence (Lat) 'discretion' 57
Prunella (Lat) 'plum-coloured' 50, 116
Psyche (Gk) 'breath of life' 80
Pyrena (Gk) 'fiery' 50, 115

Q

Queenie (Eng) 'little queen'. Also Regina, Regine 46
Quinta (Lat) 'fifth'. Also Quintina 110

R

Rabia (Arab) 'spring' 114
Rachel (Heb) 'ewe'. Also Rachele, Rachelle, Rae, Rahel,

Rakel, Raquel, Raquela, Ray, Shelley   38, 41, 50, 71, 78, 80, 95, 98, 114

Radegunde (OG) 'war-counsel'   8

Radmilla (Slav) 'worker for the people'   87

Raine (Lat) 'queen'. Also Raina   50

Ran (ON) Kindly Norse ocean goddess who rescued drowning sailors in her nets   60

Raisa (Slav) 'rose'   62

Raphaela (Heb) 'God has healed'. Also Raffaella   80, 95

Rawnie (Gipsy) 'lady'   59

Rea (Gk) 'poppy'

Rebecca (Heb) 'faithful'. Also Rebeca, Rebeka, Rebekah, Rivkah   38, 71, 78, 98

Regina (Lat) 'queen'. Also Gina, Queenie, Regan, Regine, Ríona   43, 87, 125

Renata (Lat) 'reborn'   65, 97, 112, 119

Rene (Gk) 'peace'. Also Irene   54, 62, 70

Renee (Fr) 'reborn'   41, 97

Rhea (Gk) Mother of all the Greek gods. Also Ria   47, 50, 95

Rhoda (Gk) 'rose isle'

Rhonda (OG) 'power'. Also Ronalda, Rona   60

Rhonwen (Welsh) 'slender'

Ricarda (OE) 'strong leader'. Also Rica, Riccarda, Richarda, Richelle, Richenda, Richenza, Richmal   15, 50, 80

Riccadonna (It) 'rich lady'   89

Rihana (Arab) 'sweet basil'

Rilla (OG) 'brook'   50

Rita (Fr) 'daisy'   41, 98

Roanna (Lat) compound of Rose and Anna. Also Roanne   51

Roberta (OG) 'fame-bright'. Also Roberte, Bobbie, Bobby

Robina (OG) 'fame-bright'. Also Robin, Robyn, Robynne   51, 99

Rochelle (OF) 'little rock'. Also Roche, Rochella, Rochette   95

Roisin (Lat) 'rose'. Irish form of Rose. Also Rois   78

Rokeya (Pers) 'she rises on high', 'dawn'   113

Rolanda (OG) 'famous in the land'

Romaine (Lat) 'of Rome'. Also Roma, Romana   51, 66, 95

Romola (Lat) 'of Rome'   51

Rosa (Lat) 'rose'. Also Rosebud   78

Rosabel (Lat) 'beautiful rose'   51, 97

Rosalba (Lat) 'white rose'   95, 115

Rosalind (OG) 'horse-snake', or Spanish 'lovely rose'. Also Rosalie, Rosaline, Rosalyn, Ros, Roz   98, 125

Rosamond (Lat) 'rose of the world'. Also Rosamund 10, 98

Rosana (Lat) compound of Rose and Anna. Also Roseanne   47

Rosaria (It) 'rosary', or 'rosy air'. Suitable for a baby placed in the Virgin Mary's care   98

Rose (Lat) 'rose', or Old German *hros*, 'horse'. Also Rosie, Rosy   56, 75, 112

Rosemary (Lat) compound of Rose and Mary. Also Rosemarie   56

Rosetta (Lat) 'little rose'. Also Rosina, Rosita   51, 65, 95

Rowena (OE) 'slender'. Also thought of as 'of rowans'   6, 47, 98, 116

Roxanne (Pers) 'dawn'. Also Roxanna, Roxine, Roxy 40, 112

Ruby (Lat) 'red'. A dark red jewel. Also Rubetta, Rubette, Rubi, Rubia, Rubina   55, 117

Rudy (OG) 'fame'. Also Rudella, Rudelle   75, 99

Rufina (Lat) 'red-haired'   51, 95

Rula (Lat) 'model'   51, 87

Rumer (Gipsy) 'human being', from 'rom', the Romany race, taken to mean 'gipsy'   47, 59

Rusty (Eng) 'tawny-coloured'   117

Ruth (Heb) 'vision of beauty', or English, 'compassion'   46, 71, 78

S

Saba (Heb) 'old' 51

Sabina (Lat) 'of the Sabine race' 47

Sabra (Heb) 'cactus', tender but tough 95

Sabrina (Lat) 'of the River Severn' 40

Sacha (Gk) 'defender of men'. Also Sasha 40

Sadie (Heb) 'princess'. Also Sadye, Saidee 40

Sadira (Pers) 'lotus flower' 115

Saffron (Arab) 'saffron', the costly yellow stamen of the crocus, used in cooking 95, 117

Sage (Lat) 'health'. Via English, it now means 'wise' 56

Salena (Lat) 'salty' – bracing and sassy 51

Sally (Heb) 'princess' 43, 75

Salome (Heb) 'peace of Zion'. The name of Herod's seductive dancing niece. A form of 'shalom' 95

Salvia (Lat) 'health', the fragrant herb sage 56

Samira (Arab) 'entertainer' 47

Sandra (Gk) 'defender of men'. Also Sandie, Sandy 41, 99

Sapphira (Gk) 'sapphire', the deep blue jewel. Also Sapir, Sapira, Sapphire 55, 95, 115

Sara (Heb) 'princess' 98

Sarah (Heb) 'princess'. Also Sally, Sarai, Sarice, Sarina, Sarita, Shari, Sher, Socha, Soralie 38, 46, 65, 78

Savannah (Sp) 'the dry'. Now thought of as the great roaming grasslands of Africa. Also Savanna 95

Saxona (Lat) 'of the Saxons', the ancient Germanic race who took over Britain in the fifth and sixth centuries AD 51

Scarlett (Eng) 'red' 95, 117

Sebastiane (Gk) 'venerable'. Also Sebastiana 51

Secunda (Lat) 'second girl' 109

Selina (Gk) 'moon-like'. Also Celena, Celene, Celina, Celinda, Sela, Selena, Seline 98

Selima (Arab) 'healthy'

Selma (OG) 'helmet of God'. A form of Anselma, a rare old English name. Also Arabic, 'secure'   60

Semele (Gk) lovely mortal lover of the chief Greek god Zeus   51

Septima (Lat) 'seventh'. Also seven   110

Serafina (Heb) 'burning'. Now means 'of seraphim', the chief angels at the throne of God. Also Seraphina, Seraphita   51, 65, 95

Serena (Lat) 'calm'. Also Serepta, Sirena   95, 112, 127

Sexta (Lat) 'the sixth'   110

Sharon (Heb) 'a plain'   40

Sheena (Irish) an Irish feminine of John   40, 60

Sheila (Lat) 'blind'. From the Roman gens Caecilius. Also Sheelagh, Sheelah, Sheilah, Shelagh, Shelley, Shielah, Sile   41, 75, 98

Shirley (OE) 'sunny clearing'   41

Shona (Heb) an Irish form of Jane, feminine of John. Also Shaina, Shaine, Shana, Shayne, Shonie, Sinead   60

Sian (Heb) 'Jehovah has favoured', a Welsh form of Jane   78

Sibylla (Gk) 'mouthpiece of the gods'. Also Cybil, Cybill, Sibel, Sibella, Sibelle, Sibilla, Sibyl, Sibylle   95

Sidonie (Lat) 'fine cloth'. Also Sidonia, Sidony

Sidney (Gk) 'follower of Dionysus'

Sidra (Lat) 'star'   51

Siena (It) Italian city   66

Signe (Lat) 'sign'   63

Sigrid (OG) 'victory'   6

Silvana (Lat) 'of the woods'   65

Silvia (Lat) 'of the woods'. Also Sylvia, Sylvie   64, 98, 125

Simone (Heb) 'aware'

Sinead (Heb) 'Jehovah has favoured'. Irish form of Jane   60

Siobhan (Heb) Irish form of Jane

Sirena (Gk) 'faithful'. Also, the tempting Sirens, bringing men to their doom for love   51

Sirios (Gk) 'bright star'

Solita (Lat) 'solitary'   111

Sophia (Gk) 'wisdom'. Also Sofia, Sophie, Zofia, Zophie   38, 47, 62, 65, 73, 98, 127

Sophronia (Gk) 'prudence'   51

Sorrel (Eng) fresh, zesty green salad plant   51, 117

Speranza (Lat) 'hope'

Spring (Eng) 'springtime'   114

Stacey (Gk) 'resurrection', a short form of Anastasia. Also Stacia, Stacie, Stacy, Stasha   40, 62, 75, 112

Stella (Lat) 'star'   127

Stephania (Gk) 'crowned'. Also Stefania, Stefanie, Steffi, Stephanie   46, 65, 118

Storm (Eng) 'storm'   95, 117

Sun (Eng) 'sunshine'. Also Sunni, Sunny, Sunshine   114

Susan (Heb) 'graceful white lily'. Also Sukey, Susie, Zsa Zsa   46, 78

Susannah (Heb) 'graceful white lily'. Also Susanna, Suzanne, Suzanna, Suzannah, Suzette, Suzi   46, 97, 98, 127

T

Tabitha (Heb) 'gazelle'   43, 73

Tacita (Lat) 'quiet'

Taddea (Heb) 'praise', the feminine of Thaddeus

Taja (Arab) 'crown'

Takara (Jap) 'precocious'

Talia (Heb) 'the lamb'

Tallulah (Native American) 'running water'. Also Tallula

Tamara (Heb) 'palm', used as a Russian name. Also Tamarind, the Indian date-palm, and Tamar, the Cornish river   47, 80, 95, 125

Tamath (Arab) 'to pace out one's own'

Tamsin (Heb) 'twin', the feminine of Thomas. Also Tam, Tamasin, Tamasine, Tammy, Tamzin, Tamzina, Thomasa, Thomasin, Thomasina 40, 73, 75, 111

Tangye (ON) 'sting', hence spicy challenging character 60

Tanith (Irish) 'heir to the chief' 60

Tanya (Slav) Possibly 'queen'. Short form of Tatiana. Also Tanhya, Tania, Titania, Tonya 95

Tara (Irish) 'rocky outcrop'. Home of Ireland's ancient high kings 41, 95

Tasarla (Gipsy) 'morning and evening' 59

Tatiana (Slav) Possibly 'little queen' 62, 95, 127

Tatum (OE) 'cheerful'

Tegan (Celt) 'doe' 60

Tempest (OF) 'stormy' 116

Tertia (Lat) 'third'. Also Terchie 109

Tessa (Lat) 'fourth girl'. Also Tessara 110

Thalassa (Gk) 'sea'

Thalia (Gk) 'flourishing bloom', the Greek muse of comedy

Thea (Gk) 'goddess'

Thelma (Gk) 'nurseling', a made-up literary name 124

Theodora (Gk) 'gift of god'. Also Dora, Fedora, Fjodora, Tedra, Teodora, Teodosia, Theodosia

Theophilia (Gk) 'beloved of God'. Also Offie, Offy, Theophila, Tiffany 15, 97

Thera (Gk) 'untamed' 51

Theresa (Gk) 'reaper', or 'from Tharasia'. Also Teresa, Terese, Teresina, Teresita, Teressa, Tereza, Terry, Therese 63, 98, 99, 117

Thetis (Gk) The beautiful sea-nymph mother of Achilles

Thomasina (Heb) 'twin'. With Thomasa, the feminine of Thomas 73, 111

Thora (ON) 'thunderer'. Feminine form of Thor, the god of thunder 60, 111, 117

Tierney (Irish) 'grandchild of chiefs'

Tilly (OG) 'battle-strength', a short form of Matilda. Also
    Tilda, Tildi, Tildie, Tillie   46

Timothea (Gk) 'honour to God'. Feminine form of
    Timothy

Topaza (Gk) 'topaz', a gemstone. Also Topaz   55, 117

Tracey (Gk) 'reaper', or 'from Tharasia'. A diminutive of
    Theresa. Also Tracy   40, 97

Trixie (Lat) 'bringer of joy', a diminutive of Beatrix   40,
    75

Trudy (OG) 'spear-strength', a short form of Gertrude.
    Also Trudi   41, 75

Tuesday (ON) 'day of Tiw, son of Odin'   111

Twyla (Eng) 'twill-weave'. Also Twila

U

Ulla (Lat) 'little she-bear'   63

Ulricka (OE) 'little ruler of wolves'. Also Ulrica, Ulricha,
    Ulrika, Ulrike   63

Ultima (Lat) 'the utmost'   111

Una (Lat) 'one'. Also a variant of Oonagh   111

Unity (Lat) 'oneness'

Ursula (Lat) 'little she-bear'. Also Orsa, Orsola, Ursa,
    Ursala, Ursina, Ursine, Ursulina   8, 71, 125

V

Valda (ON) 'battle-heroine'   60

Valentina (Lat) 'strong, healthy'. The name has sub-
    sequently become associated with romantic power.
    Also Val, Vale, Valeda, Valencia, Valentia, Valera,
    Valida, Vallie, Tina   51, 95

Valerie (Lat) 'strong, healthy'. French form of
    Valentina   98

Vanessa (Eng) Literary name made up by Jonathan Swift 41, 71, 73, 124

Venezia (It) Name of the beautiful canal city on the sea. Also Venetia, Venice 66, 73, 80, 95

Venus (Lat) 'love', the goddess of Love 95

Vera (Lat) 'true', Slav 'faith'. Also Verena, Verina 51

Verda (Lat) 'young, fresh' 114

Verity (Lat) 'truth' 57

Veronica (Lat) 'true image'. Also Veronika, Veronique, Vroni 98

Vespera (Gk) 'evening' 51

Vesta (Lat) 'goddess of the hearth'. Also Hesta, Hesther

Victoria (Lat) 'victorious'. Also Vicky, Vikki, Viktoria, Viktorine, Vita, Vitoria, Vittoria, Vittorina 46, 73, 75

Victorine (Lat) 'conqueror'

Viola (Lat) 'violet'. Also Vi, Violante, Viole 56, 95, 98, 114, 125

Violet (Lat) 'violet'. Also Violetta, Violette, Vye 56, 97, 98, 114, 127

Virginia (Lat) 'maidenly'. Also Ginger, Ginny, Verginia, Virginie 4, 71, 73, 75, 98

Vita (Lat) 'victorious'. Short form of Victoria 51, 80, 112

Vivien (Lat) 'lively'. Also Bibiana, Fithian, Viv, Viveca, Vivi, Vivian, Viviana, Vivienne, Vyvyan 97, 99, 112

W

Wallis (OE) 'wall'

Wanda (OG) 'slender staff'. Also Vanda, Wanaka 60

Wendy (Eng) Name made up by J. M. Barrie in *Peter Pan* 41, 98, 124

Wilhelmina (OG) 'helmet of resolution'. Feminine form
   of William. Also Billie, Guglielma, Guillelmine,
   Guillema, Helma, Vilma, Wilhelma, Willamina,
   Wilma   15

Willow (Eng) 'willow'   56, 117

Winifred (OG) 'peaceful friend'. Also Freda, Freddy,
   Venefrida, Wenefrede, Winefred, Win, Winifrid,
   Winnie, Wynne   8, 43, 71, 75

Winona (Native American) 'first daughter'. A Sioux
   name   109

X

Xenia (Gk) 'hospitable'   127

Y

Yasmin (Pers) 'jasmine flower'. Also Yasmine   41, 97

Yolande (Lat) 'violet'

Yule (OE) 'Christmas-born'   118

Yvette (OG) 'yew'   97

Yvonne (OG) 'yew'   98

Z

Zarah (Heb) 'princess'   112

Zea (Gk) 'grain'   117

Zerlinda (Heb) 'beautiful dawn'. Also Zelinda, Zorina
   112

Zeta (Heb) 'olive'. Also Zetana, Zetta, Zita   110

Zilla (Heb) 'shade'. Also Zila, Zillah, Zilli   118

Zinnia (Lat) Flower named after botanist Johann Zinn
   (1727–59)   56, 95

Zipporah (Heb) 'bird'   13
Zoe (Gk) 'life'   98, 112, 114
Zuleika (Arab) 'peace'. Potiphar's biblical wife. Also
  Zuelia   51

Glossary of Boys' Names

Note The following abbreviations are used throughout the Glossary:

(Af) African
(Arab) Arabic
(Celt) Celtic
(Dan) Danish
(Eng) Modern English
(Fr) Modern French
(Ger) Modern German
(Gk) Greek
(Haw) Hawaiian
(Heb) Hebrew
(It) Italian
(Jap) Japanese

(Lat) Latin
(Native American) American Indian
(OE) Old English
(OF) Old French
(OG) Old German
(ON) Old Norse
(Pers) Persian
(San) Sanskrit
(Scot) Scots Gaelic
(Slav) Slavonic
(Sp) Spanish
(Welsh) Welsh

It's a boy!

A

Aaron (Heb) 'enlightened'. Also Ahron, Aron, Haroun

Abel (Heb) 'breath'. Also Abe 13, 44, 48, 87, 104, 112

Abelard (OG) 'noble'. Also Abbey, Abe 51

Abner (Heb) 'father of light'

Abraham (Heb) 'father of multitudes'. Also Avrum, Bram, Ham

Absalom (Heb) 'father of peace' 13

Achilles (Gk) Sulky but glamorous Greek hero of the Trojan war. Also Achille, Achilleus

Adam (Heb) 'man of the red earth' 38, 104, 125

Adolph 'noble-wolf'. Also Adolf, Adolphus 15

Adlai (Heb) 'my witness' 85

Adrian (Lat) 'dark', 'of the Adriatic'. Also Adriano, Adrien, Arrien, Hadrian 42, 64, 78, 103, 113, 125

Aegir (ON) Norse god of the sea 61

Aelfric (OE) 'elf-rule', wise and quick-witted. Also Alfric 51

Aeneas (Gk) 'renowned one'. Trojan hero who founded Rome. Also Angus, Aonghus, Eneas 51

Aidan (Irish) 'little fiery one'. Also Adan, Eden 8, 12, 48, 104, 113

Aiken (OE) 'oaken'. Also Aickin, Aikin 51

Alan (Celt) 'handsome'. Also Alean, Ailin, Alain, Aland, Alano, Alein, Allan, Allen, Alleyn 42, 64, 78, 103

Alard (OG) 'hard and noble'. Also Adlard, Alart, Allard 8, 51

Alaric (OG) 'noble-hard'. Also Alarick, Alarico, Alarik 6, 51

Alastair (Gk) 'defender of men'. Scots form of Alexander. Also Alistair 58, 78

Alban (Lat) 'white'. Also Albion, Alwin, Aubin, Aubyn 8, 12, 48, 104

Alberic (OG) 'clever ruler'. Also Aubrey, Avery, Oberon 51

Albert (OG) 'noble and famous'. Also Aubert 103, 128

Aldous (OG) 'old'. Also Aldan, Aldhem, Aldo, Eldon, Elton 6, 8, 12, 48, 51

Aldred (OE) 'old-counsel' 6, 51

Aldrich (OG) 'old and powerful'. Also Aldric, Audric 87

Aldwin (OE) 'old wise friend'. Also Aldan, Eldwin 6, 51

Alexander (Gk) 'defender of men'. Also Alec, Alejandro, Alejo, Alek, Aleksander, Aleksandr, Aleksei, Alesaunder, Alessander, Alessandro, Alex, Alexandre, Alexei, Alexis, Alexius, Alick, Alisander, Alisandre, Alisaunder, Allesandro, Elexander, Sacha, Sandro, Sandy, Sasha, Saunders 38, 42, 46, 62, 64, 71, 73, 78, 104, 128

Alfred (OE) 'elf-counsel'. Also Alfeo, Alfie, Alfio, Alfredo, Alfrid, Alfris, Fred 6, 17, 103, 127

Algernon (OF) 'bewhiskered'. Also Algar, Alger, Algie, Algy 9, 11, 51, 73

Alonzo (OG) 'noble' 125

Aloysius (OG) 'glorious battle'

Alphonse (OG) 'noble and eager'

Alvin (OG) 'noble friend'. Also Alwyn 6, 51, 87, 106

Amadeus (Lat) 'beloved of God'. Also Amadeo, Amado, Amando 81

Ambrose (Gk) 'divine'. Also Ambrogi, Ambros, Ambrosio 8, 70, 81, 104

Amfrid (OG) 'peace of the forefathers' 6

Amory (Lat) 'love' 51

Anders (Gk) 'manly' 63

Andrew (Gk) 'manly'. Also Andre, Andrea, Andrei, Andrej, Andreas, Andres, Andy, Drew 12, 46, 62, 64, 103

Aneurin (Lat) 'honourable'. Also Nye 61

Angel (Gk) 'messenger'. Also Angelo   87, 118, 125

Angus (Scot) 'the only choice'   58, 61, 104, 119

Anselm (OG) 'helmet of God'. Also Anselmo, Anzelm, Elmo   8, 12, 62, 81

Antony (Lat) 'priceless', of the Roman clan Antonius. Also Anton, Anthony, Antoine, Antonio, Tony   12, 42, 46, 64, 78, 81, 103, 125

Archard (OE) 'bowman'   51

Archibald (OG) 'truly brave'. Also Archie   9, 54

Arden (Lat) 'burning, ardent'   116

Ariel (Heb) 'lion of God'. A name of Jerusalem, and the quicksilver spirit who appears in Shakespeare's *The Tempest*   51

Aristo (Gk) 'best'. Also Ari, Aristos, Aristotle   65

Arnold (OG) 'eagle-strong'. Arnie, Arno   54, 63, 64, 106

Arthur (Welsh) 'bear'. Art, Artair, Arte, Artois, Artur, Arturo, Artos, Artus   54, 103, 125

Asa (Heb) 'healer'   86

Ashley (OE) 'meadow of ash-trees'. Also Ash

Auberon (OG) 'little elf-ruler'. Also Oberon, Bron   51, 81

Aubrey (OG) 'elf-ruler'. Also Avery   48, 73, 81

Audun (ON) 'desert-space'   63

Augustine (Lat) 'venerable'. Also Aguistin, Agustin, Augustin, Austen, Austin, Gus   9, 12, 44, 104

Augustus (Lat) 'majestic'. Agosto, August, Auguste, Augusto, Gus   4, 15, 48

Aurelian (Lat) 'golden'. Also Aurelio, Aurelius   4, 15

Axel (OG) 'father of peace'. Also Aksel, Ax, Axe   102

Aylmer (OE) 'noble and famous'. Also Aylmar, Aymar, Elmer   17

B

Badhur (Arab) 'born at full moon'   113

Bal (Gipsy) 'hair'   59

Balder (ON) The Norse god of peace and light   61

Baldric (OG) 'bold ruler'   9, 51

Baldwin (OG) 'bold friend'. Also Balduin, Baudoin, Win   51

Baptist (Gk) 'to dip'. Also Baptista, Baptiste, Battista   51, 125

Bardolf (OG) 'bright wolf'. Also Bardolph, Bardy. One of Prince Hal's wild drinking chums in *Henry IV Part I*   9, 51, 125

Barnabas (Heb) 'son of consolation'. Also Barnaby, Barney, Barnum   1, 2, 44, 76, 81, 104

Barnet (OG) 'bear-hard'   51

Barry (Irish) 'spear'. Also Barret, Barrie   9, 40, 102

Bartholomew (Heb) 'son of a farmer'. Also Bart, Bartel   9, 12, 44, 102, 104

Basil (Gk) 'kingly'. Also Basile, Basilio, Basilius, Vassily, Baz   12, 58, 71, 73, 104

Bavol (Gipsy) 'air, wind'   59

Bayard (Lat) 'tawny'   51

Bede (OE) 'prayer'   8, 12, 48, 104

Benedict (Lat) 'blessing'. Also Ben, Benedick, Benet, Benito   9, 12, 38, 44, 78, 104, 125

Benjamin (Heb) 'son of my right hand'. Also Ben   38, 46, 71, 81, 104

Bernard (OG) 'bear-hard'. Also Barnard, Barnet, Berne, Bernardo, Bernhard, Burnard   10, 12, 42, 51, 71, 78, 103, 104

Bersh (Gipsy) 'yearling'. Also Besh   59

Bertram (OG) 'bright raven'. Also Bartram, Bert, Bertran, Bertrand, Bertrando, Bertrem, Burt   10, 58, 81, 102, 113, 125

Beverley (OE) 'from the brook of beavers'. Also Bevis   10, 51, 106

Bjorn (OG) 'bear'. A Norse name   63

Blake (ON) 'gleaming white'   40

Blase (Gk) 'stammering'. Also Blasius, Blaise, Blaze   51

Boniface (Lat) 'doer of good'   86

Bor (Gipsy) 'hedgerow'   59

Boris (Slav) 'fighter'. Also Borys   62, 127

Bowle (Gipsy) 'snail'   59

Bradley (OE) 'broad clearing'. Also Brad, Bradleigh, Brady, Lee, Leigh   76

Brage (ON) son of Odin, the chief god of Norse mythology. Also Braggo, Bragi   61

Bram (Heb) 'father of multitudes'. Also Abraham   44, 48, 104

Bran (Celt) 'raven'   113

Brand (OE) 'fiery torch'. Also Brandon   6, 61, 113

Brendan (Irish) 'stinking hair'. Also Brennan, Bryn   104

Brent (OE) 'steep hill'   42

Brett (OF) 'Breton'

Brewster (OE) 'ale-maker'   44, 51, 104

Brian (Celt) 'strength'. Also Briano, Briant, Brion, Bryan, Bryant, Bryon   10, 42, 106

Brishan (Gipsy) 'child born in the rain'   59

Brock (OE) 'badger'   48, 85, 102

Broderick 'son of Roderick'. Also Brody   42

Bruce (OF) 'of the woodland'   42, 106

Bruno (OE) 'brown'   48, 64, 104, 117

Brutus (Lat) The name of 'the noblest Roman of them all'   4, 51, 102, 125

C

Cadmus (Gk) The founder-king of Thebes in Greek mythology   51, 112

Cadoc (Welsh) 'warlike one'   51, 61

Cadwallader (Welsh) 'war-leader'   61

Cai (Lat) of the Roman gens of Caius. Also Kay   61

Caius (Lat) of the Roman gens of Caius   4, 125

Caleb (Heb) 'dog'. Also Cal   44

Calum (Lat) 'dove', a Celtic name. Also Callum, Colm, Colum, Columba, Malcolm   48, 61, 104

Calvin (Lat) 'bald'   11, 71, 85

Cameron (Scot) 'crooked nose'   88

Camlo (Gipsy) 'lovely'   59

Campbell (Scot) 'crooked mouth'   87

Canute (ON) 'race'. Also Knut. Name of the great but humble Danish king who commanded the waves to cease in an effort to show his over-smarmy courtiers that he was not all-powerful   6, 86

Cappi (Gipsy) 'prosperity'   59, 76

Caradoc (Welsh) 'amiable'. Also Caractacus, Caratacos, Carthac   51, 61

Carl (OG) 'man'. Also Carlo, Carlos   40, 48, 64, 102

Carol (OG) 'man'   106

Casimir (Slav) 'peace-ruler'. Also Kasimir, Kazmer   62

Caspar (OG) 'imperial'. One of the Three Wise Men. Also Casper   113, 118

Cassius (Lat) 'vain'. Also Case, Casey, Cash, Cass, Cassio   4, 146

Cecil (Lat) 'blind', from the noble Roman Caecilius clan   73, 106

Cedric (Welsh) 'war chief'. Also Cerdic   6, 71, 106, 123

Cesare (Lat) 'blue-grey', but means 'imperial', since Gaius Julius Caesar made the name his own   127

Chad (OE) 'warlike'   44, 51, 102

Charles (OG) 'manly'. Also Carl, Carlo, Carlos, Cary, Charlie, Chuck, Karel, Karl, Karol   38, 46, 76, 78, 103, 129

Chauncey (Lat) 'happenstance'. Also Chance, Chancey, Chaune   88

Chester (Lat) 'fort'

Chiel (OE) 'lad'. Also Chal, Chelovik   61

Chik (Gipsy) 'earth'   59, 76

Christian (Lat) 'Christian'. Also Cristian, Kristian, Kristion   48, 63, 73, 104, 127

Christmas (Eng) 'Christmas-born'   118

Christopher (Gk) 'bearer of Christ'. Also Chris, Christoffer, Christoforo, Christoph, Christophe, Christy, Cris, Cristobal, Cristoforo, Christos, Cristoval, Kester, Kit, Kristoff   38, 45, 65, 71, 78, 103

Cicero (Lat) 'chick-pea'   88

Clarence (Lat) 'bright'   71, 73, 106, 113

Claude (Lat) 'lame'. Also Claud, Claudio, Claudios, Claudius, Klaudio, Klaudius   4, 65, 71, 126

Clay (OE) 'clay'. Also Clayton, Cletus   44, 86, 102, 104

Clement (Lat) 'kind'. Also Clem, Clemens, Kliment, Klimt   44, 51, 64, 71, 104

Clifford (OE) 'cliff ford'. Also Cliff

Clint (OE) 'from the headland steading'. Also Clinton   102

Clive (OE) 'at the cliff'   18, 58, 78

Clovis (Lat) 'renowned warrior'   51, 71, 81

Cody (OE) 'cushion', but more usually used in memory of 'Buffalo Bill' Cody

Colan (Lat) 'dove', a Cornish name

Colin (Gk) 'victory of the people'   42

Colum (Lat) 'dove'. Also Colm, Columba

Colwyn (Welsh) 'hazel-grove'   61

Conal (Irish) 'high and mighty', an Irish name   61

Conan (Celt) 'high and competent'. Also Conant, Conn, Connor, Kynan   61

Conor (Irish) 'noble passion'   61

Conrad (OG) 'bold counsellor'. Also Konrad   64, 71, 103

Constantine 'faithful'. Also Constantin, Constant, Costa, Costin, Konstantin   62, 65

Corin (Gk) 'youth'   126

Cormac (Irish) 'charioteer'   51

Cornelius (Lat) 'horn'. From an august Roman clan. Also Cornel   4, 71, 126

Corwin (Lat) 'friend of the heart'   86

Cory (Gk) 'helmet'

Cosmo (Gk) 'universal harmony'   65

Courtenay (OF) 'short nose'. Also Courtney 18, 106

Craig (Celt) 'of the crags' 40, 102

Crispin (Lat) 'curly-haired'. Also Crispian, Crispianus 11, 48, 71, 81, 85, 104

Curtis (Lat) 'of the court', or 'short-hose'. Also Curt 40, 102, 126

Cuthbert (OE) 'famous-bright' 6, 51, 104, 113

Cyprian (Lat) 'of Cyprus' 12, 51, 81

Cyril (Gk) 'lordly' 12, 71, 73, 106

Cyrus (Pers) 'throne' 51, 116

D

Dag (ON) 'bright day' 63

Dai (Heb) 'beloved' 61

Damian (Gk) 'tamer' 58, 104

Damon (Gk) 'guide' 51

Daniel (Heb) 'judge' 12, 38, 46, 71, 78

Darcy (Irish) 'dark' 113

Darius (Gk) 'wealthy'. Also Darian, Darien, Darren 40, 51, 81

Darrel (OE) 'dear'. Also Darell, Darryl, Daryl 40, 106

David (Heb) 'beloved of God'. Dafyd, Dafydd, Dai, Daveed, Daviot, Davit, Davyd, Dawud, Tavish 62, 78, 103, 129

Dean (OE) 'from the valley' 42

Declan (Irish) Meaning unknown, but a common name in Ireland

Delaney (Irish) 'dark' 61

Denis (Gk) 'follower of Dionysus'. Also Dennis, Denys, Denzil 12, 40, 42, 88, 103, 106

Derek (OG) 'ruler of the people'. Also Dedrik, Deric, Derrick, Dirk 40

Dermot (Irish) 'envy-free'. Also Dermott, Diarmid, Diarmit, Diarmuid 61, 79

Desideratus (Lat) 'longed-for boy' 119

Desmond (Irish) 'from south Munster' 42, 106

Dickon (OE) 'hard-ruler'. Short form of Richard. Also Diccon 44, 104

Digby (OE) 'from the moated settlement' 44, 104

Diggory (OF) 'strayed'. Used as a nickname for Richard 44, 104

Dimitri (Gk) 'follower of Demeter', the fertility goddess. Also Dmitri 62, 65

Dion (Gk) 'follower of Dionysos' 126

Dolph (OG) 'noble-wolf', a short form of Adolph 102

Dominic (Lat) 'of the Lord'. Also Domenico, Domingo, Dominick, Dominique 71, 79, 104, 111

Donald (Scot) 'world-ruler'. Also Donal, Donalt 42, 103

Donatus (Lat) 'God-given'. Also Don, Donat, Donatas, Donato 14, 42, 119

Donovan (Irish) 'dark warrior'. Also Don 42

Dorian (Gk) 'from the Doric region'. Also Dorjan 51, 63, 81

Dougal (Scot) 'dark stranger'. Also Doug, Doyle 58, 61, 104

Douglas (Scot) 'from the dark water'. Also Doug, Dougie, Douglass, Duggie 18, 58, 73, 79, 103

Drake (Gk) 'serpent'. Also Draco

Drew (Gk) 'manly'. Short form of Andrew

Drogo (OG) 'to carry' 51, 102

Dudley (OE) 'from Dudda's meadow' 18, 42, 106

Dugald (Scot) 'dark stranger' 61

Duke (Lat) 'leader' 102

Dukker (Gipsy) 'bewitcher'. Also Durriken 59

Duncan (Scot) 'dark warrior' 48, 104, 126

Dunstan (OE) 'from the brown stone hill'. Also Dustin 6, 12, 48, 51, 104

Durrant (Lat) 'endurer'. Also Durand 10

Durril (Gipsy) 'berry' 59

Dwight (OF) Meaning unknown. Possibly 'from Wight'
Dylan (Welsh) 'from the sea'

E

Eamon (OE) 'rich protector'. Irish form of Edmund. Also
  Eamonn   42
Earl (OE) 'nobleman'   102
Ebenezer (Heb) 'stone of help'   13, 54, 129
Edgar (OE) 'rich spear'   6, 17, 52, 71, 73, 126
Edmund (OE) 'rich guardian'. Also Eadmond, Edmon,
  Edmond, Edmondo   6, 48, 89, 104, 126
Edred (OE) 'rich counsel'   6, 17, 52
Edric (OE) 'rich ruler'. Also Ed, Rick, Rik   52
Edward (OE) 'rich protector'. Also Edouard, Eduard,
  Eduardo, Edvard, Edwold, Duarte, Ed, Ned, Ted   38,
  45, 52, 64, 73, 75, 79, 103
Edwin (OE) 'rich friend'. Also Ed, Wyn   6, 17, 71
Egbert (OE) 'bright sword'   12, 54, 106
Egmont (OE) 'holding the mountain'. Also Egerton   52
Egon (OE) 'strong'. Also Egan, Keegan   52
Eldon (OE) 'old'. Also Aldous, Edlen, Edlon, Elton   52
Eldwin (OE) 'old friend'   52
Elvis (ON) 'elf-friend'
Emanuel (Heb) 'God is with us'. Also Emmanuel,
  Imanuel
Emery (OG) 'powerful ruler'. Also Emerick, Emlyn,
  Emory   10, 52
Enoch (Heb) 'dedicated'. Son of the murderer Cain and
  father of the ancient Methuselah   13
Eric (ON) 'honourable ruler'. Also Erik   54, 63, 71
Ernest (OG) 'earnest'. Also Ernestin, Ernesto, Ernestus,
  Ernst, Emo   54, 62, 63, 64, 71
Errol (OE) 'army strength'. A variant of Harold
Esmund (OE) 'gracious shelter'   52

Ethelred (OE) 'noble counsel' 17

Etienne (Gk) 'crowned' 64

Euan (Scot) 'youthful warrior' 79

Eugene (Gk) 'of good stock'. Also Eugen, Eugenio, Eugenius, Gene 64, 71, 73

Eustace (Gk) 'abundant corn'. Also Eustache, Eustis, Eustazio, Stacy 10, 106

Evelyn (OF) 'hazel'. Also Evel, Evelio, Evelle 73, 106, 115

Everard (OG) 'wild boar'. Also Averitt, Devereux, Eberle, Ewart 52

Ewan (Welsh) The Welsh form of John. Also Eoghan, Eoin, Evan, Evin, Evo, Owen

Ezekiel (Heb) 'may God strengthen'

F

Fabian (Lat) 'bean-grower'. Also Fabius 4, 52, 81, 104, 126

Farrel (Irish) 'heroic'. Also Farrell 61

Farquhar (Scot) 'friendly man' 52, 61

Faustus (Lat) 'fortunate' 4

Felix (Lat) 'fortunate'. Also Feliciano 4, 58, 81, 89, 104

Feodor (Gk) 'gift of God' 62

Ferdinand 'wild and warlike' 126

Fergus (Scot) 'choice of man'. Also Feargus 48, 61, 104, 119

Ferrand (OG) 'adventurer'. Also Ferrando 127

Festus (Lat) 'merry'. Also Feste 52, 126

Fidel (Lat) 'faith'. Also Fidelio

Fingal (Irish) 'fair stranger' 48, 52, 61, 104

Finn (Irish) 'blond and fair'. Also Finian, Finnegan, Finnian, Fionn 48, 52, 61, 63, 104

Fitz (OE) 'son' 76, 102

Flavian (Lat) 'blond'. Also Flavius 81

Fletcher (OE) 'arrow-maker' 81, 104
Florian (Lat) 'flowering' 52, 81
Flyn (Irish) 'son of the red-haired man' 61
Fordel (Gipsy) 'forgive' 59
Francis (OG) 'a Frank'. Also Ffransis, Francesco, Francisco, Francois, Franek, Frank, Frans, Frants, Franz, Franziskus, Pancho 44, 62, 64, 71, 73, 79, 103
Franklin (OG) 'freeman' 89
Fraser (Fr) 'strawberry-gatherer' 116
Frederick (OE) 'peace-rule'. Also Federico, Frederico, Fred, Frederic, Frederich, Frederik, Fredric, Fredrick, Friedrich, Fritz, Rick, Rik 44, 64, 76, 79, 102, 103, 126, 127
Frey (ON) 'noble man'. Frey was the Norse god of peace and fertility 52, 61, 89, 104
Fulke (OE) 'the people'. Also Fulk 10, 52, 102
Fyodor (Gk) 'gift of God' 128

G

Gabbo (ON) 'to scoff' 61
Gabriel (Heb) 'strong man of God'; the archangel 44, 52, 71, 81, 104, 128
Gael (Welsh) 'Irishman' 61
Gaius (Lat) 'rejoice'. Name of Roman family 4
Galahad (Welsh) 'war hawk' 17, 52, 61
Galen (Gk) 'tranquil' 52
Galvin (Irish) 'sparrow' 116
Gamal (Arab) 'handsomeness' 52
Gareth (Welsh) 'gentle'. Also Garth 17, 42, 61
Garret (OG) 'spear-hard'. Also Garrett 43, 52, 89
Garridan (Gipsy) 'you hid' 52, 59
Garwood (OE) 'from the fir-tree forest' 118
Gaston (Fr) 'man from Gascony' 52
Gavin (Welsh) 'white hawk'. Also Gawain, Gawen 40, 52, 61, 89

Geoffrey (OG) Meaning confused. Also Geoffroi, Geoffroy, Jeffrey 10, 45, 79, 103

George (Gk) 'farmer'. Georg, Georges, Giorgio, Joran, Jorge, Jorgen, Saoirse, Sior, Yeorgi, Yorick 46, 64, 65, 73, 79, 103, 128, 129

Geraint (Gk) 'old'. Also Gerontius 17, 52, 61

Gerald (OG) 'spear-ruler'. Also Gearalt, Gerrold, Gerry, Giraldo, Jerry 10, 46, 71, 75, 79, 103, 126

Gerard (OE) 'spear-hard'. Also Gearard, Gerardo, Geraud, Gerhard, Gerhardt, Gherardo, Gerrard, Gerry, Jerry 10, 58, 73, 75, 105

Gervase (OG) 'loyal spearman'. Also Gervais, Gervaise, Gervasio, Gervaso, Gervasius, Jarvis 10, 48

Gideon (Heb) 'destroyer' 106

Gifford (OE) 'bold giver'. Also Giff, Giffard, Gifferd, Gilroy 52

Gilbert (OE) 'shining promise'. Also Gilberto, Guilbert 10, 71, 73, 112

Giles (Gk) 'shield-bearer' 46, 74, 105, 112

Gillie (Gipsy) 'song' 59

Glenn (OE) 'valley'. Also Glen, Glyn, Glynn 40, 42

Godfrey (OE) 'God's peace'. Also Godefroi, Gottfrid 10, 54, 71

Godric (OE) 'good ruler'. Also Goodrich 52

Godwin (OE) 'good friend'. Also Goodwin, Win, Wyn 6, 52

Gordon (Scot) 'by the great hill'. Also Gordion 18, 42, 52, 71, 103

Graham (OE) 'from the grey village'. Also Graeme, Graemer, Graenum, Gram 42, 79

Grant (Fr) 'big' 42

Granville (Fr) 'from the large town'. Also Greville 18, 75

Gregory (Gk) 'watchman'. Also Greer, Greg, Gregoire, Gregor, Greggor, Gregorio, Gregorius, Grigori, Grigorio, Grischa 10, 62, 64, 71, 103

Griffin (Lat) 'griffin'. Also Gryphon   52, 102

Griffith (Welsh) 'fierce lord'. Also Griff, Gruffydd   52, 61, 102, 126

Griswald (OG) 'from the grey forest'. Also Gris, Griz   52

Gunnar (ON) 'warrior'. Also Gunner, Guntar, Gunter, Gunther   61, 63, 64

Gustave (OG) 'cudgel of the Goths'. Also Gus, Gustaf, Gustav, Gustavus   15, 44, 63, 76, 105

Guthrie (OG) 'war hero'   89

Guy (OG) 'guide'. Also Guido   10, 17, 46, 75, 105

H

Haakon (ON) 'useful'. Also Hacon, Hakon   52, 61, 105

Hadrian (Lat) 'dark' or 'of the Adriatic'   4, 52

Halcyon (Gk) 'kingfisher'   116

Ham (Heb) 'hot'

Hamish (Eng) from the Irish Seamus, pseudo-Scots for James   46, 61, 79

Hans (Lat) German form of John. Also Heinz, Honus   63, 64

Harald (OE) 'army-power'. Also Araldo, Errol, Hal, Harold, Harry, Herold   54, 89, 103

Harlequin (OE) the god Odin, or the *commedia dell'arte* character famed for his quick wit and rainbow costume. Also Quin, Quinn   81

Harvey (OG) 'warrior'   10, 129

Hector (Gk) 'steadfast'. Hector was the dashing Prince of Troy. Also Ector, Ettore   52, 75, 81, 129

Henry (OG) 'home-ruler'. Also Arrigo, Enrico, Enrique, Hal, Hank, Harry, Heindrich, Heinrich, Heinz, Hendrik, Henne, Henri, Henrik   10, 38, 45, 64, 75, 79, 103, 105, 126, 129

Herbert (OE) 'glorious soldier'. Also Eberto, Harbert   10, 106

Hereward (OE) 'army protection'. Name of Hereward the Wake, the last Saxon hero to stand against the Normans. Also Herry, Ward 6, 52

Herman (OG) 'army-man'. Also Armand, Armando, Armant 10

Hilary (Lat) 'cheerful'. Also Hilaire, Hilar, Hilarid, Hilario, Hillard, Hillary, Hillery, Hilliard, Ilario 58, 74

Hildebrand (OG) 'sword of war'. Also Hilbrand

Hobart (OG) 'bright-minded'. Also Hob, Bart 52, 105

Homer (Gk) 'promise'. Also Omer, Omero

Horace (Lat) 'keeper of the hours'. A famous Roman clan 71, 75, 106

Horatio (Lat) 'keeper of the hours', of the Roman Horatius family. Also Horace, Horacio, Horatius, Orazio 52, 74, 106, 126

Howard (OE) 'hay-warden' 18, 42

Hubert (OG) 'bright-minded'. Also Bertie, Hobard, Hobart, Umberto 71, 106

Hugh (OE) 'intelligent'. Also Hew, Hewe, Hugues, Huw, Ugo 17, 45, 74, 79, 113

Hugo (OE) 'intelligent'. A latinised form of Hugh 10, 58, 74, 102

Humphrey (OG) 'peaceful Hun' 10, 54, 71, 106

Hywel (Welsh) 'notable'. Also Howell, the English form

I

Iago (Heb) 'supplant'. A Spanish and Welsh form of James 126

Iain (Heb) 'Jehovah has favoured'. A Scots form of John. Also Ian 46, 79

Ignatius (Lat) 'fiery'. Also Iggy, Ignace, Ignacio, Ignacius, Ignaz, Ignazio, Inigo 52

Igor (ON) 'of the god Ing'. Russian form of a Norse name referring to the peace-god Frey under his name of Ing 62

Ingram (ON) 'raven of Ing'. Also Ingamar, Ingemar, Inglis, Ingmar, Ingvar, Inigo, Ingra, Ingrim 52, 61, 63, 81

Irvin (OE) 'friend of the sea'. Also Earven, Ervin, Erwin, Irvine, Irving, Irwin, Irwyn 106

Isaac (Heb) 'he laughs'. Also Ike, Isac, Isacco, Isak, Izak, Zack, Zak 47

Isidore (Gk) 'gift of Isis'. Also Dory, Isadore, Isador, Isidoro, Isidro 52

Ivan (Heb) 'Jehovah has favoured'. Russian variant of John. Also Yvan, Yvon 62

Ivar (ON) 'yew' or 'yew-bow archer'. Also Iver 52, 61

Ivo (ON) 'yew' or 'archer'. Also Ia, Yves 10, 75, 105

Ivor (Lat) 'ivory'. Also Ivair 79

J

Jack (Heb) 'Jehovah has favoured' and 'supplanter'. Short form of John and James 38, 45, 76, 105, 129

Jacob (Heb) 'supplanter'. Also Cob, Giacobo, Jacques, Jacquino, Jake, Jakob 8, 64, 71, 126, 127

Jake (Heb) 'supplanter'. Short form of Jacob and James 38, 44, 76, 105, 127

James (Heb) 'supplanter'. Also Diego, Giacomo, Hamish, Iago, Jago, Jaime, Jamey, Jamie, Jay, Jem, Jim, Seamus, Seumas, Shamus 12, 45, 74, 76, 79, 81, 102, 103, 105, 130

Jan (Heb) 'Jehovah has favoured'. Dutch and Slavic form of John. Also Janek, Janos 62

Jarek (Slav) 'of January' 62

Jarvis (OG) 'spear-vassal' 52, 105

Jason (Gk) 'healer'. Also Jasen, Jasun 38, 86, 106

Jasper (Arab) 'jasper', a quartz. Anglicised version of

Caspar, the name of one of the Three Kings of the Nativity. Also Jaspar   58, 81, 118

Jed (Arab) 'hand'   44

Jedidiah (Heb) 'beloved of the Lord'. Also Didi, Jed, Jedd, Jedediah   44

Jeffrey (OG) Meaning uncertain. A variant of Geoffrey   42

Jeremiah (Heb) 'God is exalted'. Also Geremia, Jere, Jeremias

Jeremy (Heb) 'God is exalted'. English form of Jeremiah   46, 71, 105

Jerome (Lat) 'sacred name'. Also Gerome, Geronima, Hieronymous, Jeromo, Jeronim, Jerram   12, 48, 71, 105

Jethro (Heb) 'pre-eminence'. Also Jeth   44, 52

Jevan (Heb) 'Jehovah has favoured' an anglicised Welsh form of John. Also Evan, Jevon, Owen, Sion   52

Jibben (Gipsy) 'life'. Also Jib, Jivin, Jivvil   52, 59

Joab (Heb) 'God is father'

Job (Heb) 'afflicted one'

Joachim (Heb) 'God has raised high'. Also Joaquin, Jochem, Jochen, Jock, Joe, Jokum

Jocelyn (OG) 'one of the Goths'. Also Jocelin, Joe, Joscelin, Joscelyn, Joss   10, 58

Jock (Heb) 'Jehovah has favoured', a diminutive of John, joining Jack as a name now fashionable in its own right   44, 76, 102, 130

Joel (Heb) 'Jehovah is God'

John (Heb) 'Jehovah has favoured'. Also Evan, Ewan, Ewen, Gian, Giavani, Giovanni, Hanan, Hans, Iain, Ian, Jack, Jan, Janos, Janus, Jean, Jens, Jevan, Jock, Johan, Johann, Johannes, Johnny, Jon, Jonn, Jonno, Juan, Owen, Sean, Shaughn, Shaun, Shawn, Sion, Zane   45, 64, 79, 103, 130

Jolyon (Lat) From the Roman clan of Julius   52

Jonah (Heb) 'the dove'   130

Jonas (Heb) 'doer'

Jonathan (Heb) 'Jehovah gave'. Also Gionata, Johnathan, Jonathon, Jonty, Yanaton 46, 105, 130

Jose (Heb) 'God will multiply'. A Spanish form of Joseph. Also Joseito, Pepe, Pepillo, Pepito 127

Joseph (Heb) 'God will multiply'. Also Beppo, Che, Giuseppe, Iosep, Iossif, Joe, Jose, Josef, Josephus, Jozef, Pepe, Pepin 12, 44, 76, 103, 118, 130

Josh (Heb) 'Jehovah saves'. A short form of Joshua, now appearing with Jack, Jock, Jeth and Judd as a free-standing name 38, 105

Joshua (Heb) 'Jehovah saves'. Also Josh, Joshia, Joshuah 44, 76

Josiah (Heb) 'Jehovah supports'. Also Josias 44

Joss (Celt) 'champion' 44

Joubert (OE) 'of God's radiance' 52, 116

Jovett (OE) 'of God's radiance' 52

Judd (Heb) 'praise'. Also Jud, Judah, Jude, Yehudi 44, 105

Julian (Lat) 'downy'. Of the Roman family, Julius. Also Giulio, Iulio, Jule, Jules, Julienne, Julio, Julius 46, 52, 64, 71, 105, 116

Julius (Lat) 'downy'. Of the Julian clan 4, 48, 52, 74, 81, 105, 116, 126

Junius (Lat) 'of June' 116

Justin (Lat) 'the just'. Also Giustino, Giusto, Justinian, Justino, Justis, Justus 46, 71, 81, 105

K

Kai (Lat) Welsh vestige of the Roman name Caius or Gaius 52

Kane (Irish) 'tribute'. Also Kain, Kaine 61

Kanute (ON) 'race'. Also Canute, Cnut, Cnute, Knud, Knut, Note, Nute, Nutkin 61

Karl (OG) 'man, manly'. A form of Charles. Also Carl, Carel, Karel, Karol, Karoly 62, 63, 64

Karsten (Gk) 'anointed'. Also Christian, Kristian 63

Kasimir (Slav) 'peace-ruler'. Also Casimir, Casmir 62

Kaspar (Arab) A form of Caspar, one of the Magi. Also Jaspar, Gaspar 64

Kay (Lat) Welsh corruption of the Roman name Caius or Gaius. The meaning may be 'rejoice'. Sir Kay was one of King Arthur's company of Round Table knights. Also Cai, Kai 52

Keith (Celt) 'of the forest' 42, 106

Kelvin (OE) 'lover of ships' 40, 106

Kendrick (OE) 'grand king'. Also Cynric, Ken, Kendig, Kenric 52

Kenneth (Irish) 'handsome'. Also Canice, Cennydd, Kenton 42

Kent (Celt) 'white', now largely used as the name of the area occupied by the Cantii tribe of Roman Britain from whom Kent takes its name. Also Kentigern 52, 66

Kerey (Gipsy) 'bound for home' 59

Kester (Gk) 'Christ-bearer', a diminutive of Christopher 44

Kevin (Irish) 'born handsome'. Also Caoimhain, Kev, Kevan, Keven 40, 102

Kieran (Irish) 'little dark one'. Also Ciaran, Kiernan 61

Kim (OE) 'royal', from Kimball, meaning 'royal hill' 40

Kingsley (OE) 'from the king's meadow'

Kirk (ON) 'church'. Sometimes wrongly used as a familiar of Charles 40, 102

Kistur (Gipsy) 'rider' 59

Kit (Gk) 'Christ-bearer'. Nickname for Christopher. Also Kito 44, 63, 76, 81, 105

Kwakoa (Af) 'born on Wednesday' 111

Kwame (Af) 'born on Saturday' 111

Kwasi (Af) 'born on Sunday' 111

Kyle (Irish) 'handsome' or 'from the narrow sea-channel'

L

Lachlan (Celt) 'warlike'

Laertes (Gk) The father of Odysseus, and Ophelia's brother in Shakespeare's tragedy *Hamlet* 126

Lancelot (Lat) 'spear'. Also Lance, Lancing, Lansing, Launcelot 17, 40, 52, 126

Laurence (Lat) 'bay-tree', or 'from Laurentium'. Also Larikin, Larkin, Larry, Lars, Larson, Laure, Laurens, Laurent, Laurie, Lauriston, Lauritz, Lauro, Lawrence, Lorant, Loren, Lorence, Lorens, Lorentz, Lorenz, Lorenzo, Lorin, Rance, Renzo 12, 42, 63, 64, 79, 130

Lazarus (Heb) 'God will help'. Also Lazar, Lazare, Lazaro, Lazer, Lazlo 86

Leander (Gk) 'like a lion'. Also Ander, Lea, Leandre, Leandro, Leanther, Lee, Leo 52

Lee (OE) 'from the meadow'. Also Leigh 42

Leif (ON) 'beloved'. Also Lief 61, 117

Lel (Gipsy) 'taker' 59

Leland (OE) 'meadow-land'

Lendar (Gipsy) 'from his parents' 59

Lennor (Gipsy) 'spring and summer' 59

Lensar (Gipsy) 'with his parents' 59

Leo (Lat) 'lion' 76, 81

Leofric (OE) 'loved ruler'. Also Frick 52

Leofwin (OE) 'dear friend' 52

Leon (Lat) 'lion' and a short French form of Napoleon. Also Lyon 106

Leonard (Lat) 'lion-brave'. Also Leonardo, Leoline 12, 42, 71

Leopold (Lat) 'bold for the people'. Also Leopoldo, Leupold 64, 74, 87

Leroy (Fr) 'the king'. Also Elroy, Lee, Roy

Leslie (Scot) 'low meadow' or 'garden near a pool' 106

Lester (Eng) 'from Leicester' 106

Lewis (Eng) Anglicised variant of the Welsh Lewys and the French Louis

Lex (Gk) 'word'

Liam (OG) 'helmet of resolution'. Irish form of William 61, 81

Lindsey (OE) 'from the isle of linden-trees'

Linford (OE) 'from the ford with linden-trees'

Linus (Lat) 'flaxen-haired' 52, 105

Lionel (Lat) 'little lion'. Also Lionello, Lyonel 52, 71, 74

Llewellyn (Welsh) 'lion-like'. Also Fluellan, Leoline, Llew, Llewelin

Louis (OG) 'renowned warrior'. Also Aloys, Aloysius, Clovis, Elois, Lewis, Ludeg, Ludovic, Ludvig, Ludwig, Luigi, Luis 64

Lucas (Gk) 'from Lucania'. Also Loukas, Lukas, Lukasz 52, 62, 81, 105, 113

Lucian (Lat) 'light'. Also Luciano, Lucien, Lucio, Luzian, Luzius 58, 76, 81, 126

Lucius (Lat) 'light' 4, 52

Luke (Gk) 'from Lucania'. Also Luc, Luca, Lucais, Lucano 10, 12, 44, 46, 64, 71, 81, 105, 113

Lutherum (Gipsy) 'slumber' 59

Lyndon (OE) 'from the linden-tree hill'. Also Lindon

Lysander (Gk) 'defender of men' 87, 126

M

Mabry (Celt) 'lovable', a Cornish name 61

Mac (Scot) 'son' 61

Madoc (Welsh) 'lucky'. Also Maddoc, Maddock, Maddox, Madoch 52, 61

Magnus (Lat) 'great' 52, 72

Malcolm (Scot) 'follower of St Columba'. Also Mal, Maolcolm 42, 103, 126

Mander (Gipsy) 'from myself' 59

Manfred (OG) 'man of peace'. Also Fred, Manifred

Manuel (Heb) 'God is with us'. A short form of Emmanuel 64

Marcel (Lat) 'little Marcus'. Also Marcello, Marcellus, Marzellus 48

Marcus (Lat) 'of Mars'. Also Marc, Marco, Marcos, Markos 48, 76, 81, 105

Marius (Lat) 'of Mars'. Also Mario, Marian, Marion 52, 62, 76, 81, 106

Marlon (OF) 'little falcon'. Also Marlin 106

Mark (Lat) 'of Mars', warlike 12, 46, 103

Marmaduke (Welsh) 'servant of Madoc'. Also Duke, Marmaduc, Melmidoc 52, 74, 106

Martin (Lat) 'of Mars', warlike. Also Martainn, Marten, Martijn, Martinet, Martino, Marton, Martyn, Merten, Morten 42

Marvin (OE) 'renowned friend'. Also Marven, Marwin, Merwyn 40, 106

Matthew (Heb) 'gift of God'. Also Mateo, Mateusz, Mathern, Mathias, Matias, Matok, Mattaeus, Mattathias, Matteo, Matthaus, Matthias, Matthieu, Mattieu, Mayo 10, 12, 46, 62, 72, 79, 103, 127

Mauger (OG) 'honed spear' 52

Maurice (Lat) 'man from Morocco'. Also Maur, Mauricio, Maurie, Maurise, Mauritius, Maurits, Mauriz, Maurizio, Mauro, Maurus, Maury, Morie, Moritz, Moriz, Morris 10, 71, 106

Maximilian (Lat) 'greatest'. Also Massimo, Max, Maximilien, Maximus, Maxwell 44, 75, 76, 81, 105

Maynard (OG) 'strong and hard'. Also Manard, Meinhard, Menard 10, 52

Medric (OE) 'fertile meadowland' 52

Melvin (OE) 'sword-friend'. Also Melville, Melvyn 40, 106

Merlin (Welsh) 'cliff-fort'. Marlin, Marlon, Merle, Merlo, Merlon 52, 105

Merrill (OF) 'famous'. Also Merill, Merrel, Merrell

Merrion (Welsh) Place name used as a first name, also Merryn   52, 61, 76, 105

Merripen (Gipsy) 'life and death'   59

Mervyn (OE) 'famous friend'. Also Merfyn, Mervin   42, 106

Michael (Heb) 'one like the Lord'. Also Meikle, Micah, Michal, Michel, Miguel, Mikael, Mikel, Mikhail, Mikkel, Mischa, Mitchell   12, 38, 45, 48, 62, 79, 103, 131

Miles (OG) 'beloved', or Latin 'soldier'. Also Milo, Myles   10, 58

Montgomery (OE) 'from the rich man's mountain'. Also Monty

Mordred (Lat) 'biter'. Also Modris, Modred   61

Morton (OE) 'moortown'. Also Morten   63

Mortimer (OF) 'dead sea'   52, 72, 106

N

Napoleon (Gk) 'new town'. Also Leon

Nathaniel (Heb) 'gift of God'. Also Nat, Nataniel, Nathan, Nathanael   44, 105

Nav (Gipsy) 'name'. Also Nev   59

Ned (OE) Short form of Edmund, Edward and Old English Ed family   44, 105, 131

Neil (Irish) 'champion'. Also Neal, Neils, Nels; Niadh, Nial, Niall, Niel, Niels, Nil, Niles, Nils, Nilson, Niul, Njal   42, 63, 103

Nelson (OE) 'Neil's son'

Neville (OF) 'new town'   10, 18, 58

Nicholas (Gk) 'victory of the people'. Also Claus, Cole, Collet, Klaas, Klaus, Nic, Niccolo, Nick, Nico, Nicol, Nicolai, Nicolas, Nicolaus, Nicole, Nicolo, Nike, Niki, Nikita, Nikolai, Nikolaos, Nikolas, Nikolaus, Nikolos, Nikos   12, 45, 62, 65, 76, 79, 103, 118, 130

Nigel (Irish) 'champion', the same name as Neil. Often wrongly assumed to have been derived from the Latin *niger*, meaning 'black'. Also Nidge, Nig, Nigellus, Nygall, Nye 42, 103

Ninian (Lat) 'lively'. The confused origin of this name is thought to be an early British corruption of the Latin word *vivianus* 52, 74, 112

Noel (Lat) 'Christmas-born'. Also Natale, Nollaig, Nowel, Nowell 52, 118

Norbert (OG) 'north-bright' 106

Norman (OE) 'northman'. Also Normand 54, 72

Nym (Eng) the name of one of Shakespeare's ruffians in *Henry V Part I* 126

O

Obadiah (Heb) 'servant of God'. Obadias, Obediah 13

Oberon (OG) 'little elf-ruler' 126

Octavian (Lat) 'the eighth'. Also Octavius 15, 110

Odin (ON) the chief of the Norse gods. Also Odhinn, Odon, Woden, Woten 55, 61, 63, 111

Odo (OG) 'wealthy'. Also Audo 10, 53

Odysseus (Gk) 'wanderer'

Olaf (ON) 'ancestral heritage'. Also Anleifr, Olav, Olave, Ole, Oleg, Olen, Olif, Olin 61, 62, 63

Oliver (ON) 'ancestral heritage', sometimes given as 'olive' from the Latin. Also Anleifr, Olivero, Olivier, Olivierio, Olvan 10, 38, 48, 74, 79, 105, 126

Orestes (Gk) 'mountain man' 53

Orion (Gk) 'son of fire' 53, 116

Orlando (OG) 'renowned in the land'. Also Arland, Orlan, Orland, Orlov, Roland, Rowland 64, 81, 126

Orsino (Lat) 'little bear' 126

Orson (Lat) 'bear' 53

Osbert (OE) 'god-bright' 53

Oscar (OE) 'divine spear'. Also Asgar, Ansgar, Osgar, Oskar 6, 48, 63, 81, 127

Osmand (OE) 'protected by God'. Also Esme, Osmond, Osmund 53

Osric (OE) 'divine rule' 53, 126

Oswald (OE) 'divine forest'. Also Osvald, Oswal, Oswaldo, Oswall, Oswold, Waldo 53, 74, 106

Oswin (OE) 'friend of God' 53

Otto (OG) 'wealthy'. Also Odo, Otello, Othello, Otho 76, 110, 126, 127

Ovid (Lat) 'egg' 53, 105

Owen (Heb) 'Jehovah has favoured', a Welsh form of John. Sometimes given as 'lamb' or 'noble'. Also Eoin, Eoghan, Ewen, Owain, Ywain 48, 61, 72, 105, 115, 126

P

Pablo (Lat) 'small', a Spanish form of Paul

Paddy (Lat) 'noble', a short form of Padraig or Patrick 76, 131

Padraig (Lat) 'noble', the deep Irish form of Patrick. Also Padraic

Pagan (Lat) 'countryman' 53, 105

Pal (Gipsy) 'brother' 59

Paris (Gk) prince of Troy and seducer of Helen 53, 66

Pascal (Lat) Easter. Also Paschal, Paschalis, Pasco, Pascoe, Pask, Pasquale 115

Patrick (Lat) 'noble'. Also Padraic, Padraig, Padrig, Patrice, Patrizio, Patrizius 46, 79, 103

Patrin (Gipsy) 'trailblazer' 53, 59

Pattin (Gipsy) 'leaf' 59

Paul (Lat) 'small'. Also Paavo, Pablo, Paolo, Paolino, Paulinus, Paulus, Pavel, Poul 12, 42, 79, 103, 131

Pedro (Lat) 'rock', a Spanish form of Peter 126

Pelham (OE) 'Pella's village' 18, 74

Pentecost (Gk) 'Whitsuntide' 115

Pepin (OG) 'petitioner' 53

Perceval (Fr) 'of Percheval'. Also Percival, Percy 18, 54, 106, 124

Peregrine (Lat) 'pilgrim'. Also Pellegrino, Peregrin, Perry 53, 74, 105

Perseus (Gk) 'destroyer'. Also Percy 105

Peter (Gk) 'rock'. Also Farris, Ferris, Pearce, Peder, Pedro, Per, Perkin, Perran, Perren, Petr, Petros, Petrus, Petur, Pierce, Piero, Pierre, Piers, Pieter, Pietrek, Pietro, Piotr 12, 46, 53, 63, 65, 76, 79, 103, 105, 131

Philip (Gk) 'horse-lover'. Also Felip, Felipe, Filip, Filippo, Lippo, Philipp, Philippe, Phillipus, Phillip, Pip 12, 46, 72, 74, 79, 103

Phineas (Heb) 'oracle' 53

Phoebus (Gk) 'of the sun' 116

Phoenix (Gk) 'life from ashes' 115

Pias (Gipsy) 'fun' 59

Placido (Lat) 'calm' 111

Plato (Gk) 'broad-shouldered'

Pov (Gipsy) 'earth' 59

Priam (Gk) the king of Troy 53

Primo (Lat) 'first' 109

Prospero (Lat) 'successful'. Also Prosper 89, 126

Puck (Eng) The name of the magical woodland sprite in Shakespeare's *A Midsummer Night's Dream* 126

Q

Quentin (Lat) 'the fifth'. Also Quince, Quincy, Quinn, Quintin, Quintus 17, 53, 72, 74, 102, 105, 110, 126

R

Rafael (Heb) 'God has healed'. Rafaelle, Rafaello, Raphael 64, 81, 105

Rafe (OE) 'wolf-counsel' 48, 53

Rafferty (Irish) 'rich and successful'. Also Raff 61

Ragnar (ON) 'wise soldier'

Ralph (OE) 'wolf-counsel'. Also Rafe, Raff, Ralf, Rolf, Rolph 10, 17, 48, 53, 63, 65, 74, 102, 103

Randolph (OE) 'shield-wolf'. Also Randal, Randolf 6, 74

Ranulf (OE) 'shield-wolf'. Also Ranulph 6, 53

Raoul (ON) 'wolf-counsel'. Also Raul 53, 64, 65, 74, 102

Raven (OE) 'raven', from *hraefn* 53, 102, 105

Raymond (OE) 'wise protector'. Also Raimondo, Raimund, Ramon 42, 103

Reginald (OE) 'mighty warrior'. Also Ranald, Reginauld, Regnault, Reinald, Renaldo, Reynaldo, Renaud, Rinaldo 54, 106, 126

Reid (OE) 'red-haired' 117

Remus (Lat) 'oar', swift-moving. Also Remer, Remy 53, 81

Rene (Lat) 'reborn' 112, 115, 119

Reuben (Heb) 'behold a son' 117

Rex (Lat) 'king' 40, 87, 102

Reynard (OG) 'brave and wise'. Also Ray, Raynard, Renard, Reynaud 10, 53, 105, 117

Rhys (Welsh) 'enthusiastic'. Also Race, Reece, Rhett

Richard (OG) 'powerful ruler'. Also Dickon, Rab, Ric, Ricard, Ricardo, Richart, Ricci, Rick, Rickard, Rico, Rocco 10, 40, 45, 76, 79, 89, 103, 127, 129

Riordan (Irish) 'royal poet' 81

Roarke (Irish) 'famous ruler' 61

Robert (OE) 'fame-bright'. Also Bob, Hab, Hob, Hobson, Hodge, Rab, Riobard, Roban, Robard, Robart, Robben, Roberto, Robin, Robson 45, 76, 79, 103, 129

Robin (OE) 'fame-bright', a familiar of Robert 45

Roderick (OG) 'renowned ruler'. Also Rhodric, Rod, Roderic, Roderich, Roderigo, Rodrigo, Rodrique, Roric 102, 127

Rodney (OE) 'reed island' 42, 54, 74, 106

Roger (OE) 'famous warrior'. Also Rogelio, Rogerio, Rozer, Rugero   10, 17, 45, 103, 131

Roland (OG) 'famed throughout the land'. Also Rolla, Rollan, Rollen, Rollo, Rowland   10, 17, 53, 58, 74, 102, 103, 131

Roman (Lat) 'Roman'. Also Romain, Romano, Romanus, Romeo, Romolo, Romulus   62, 126

Ronald (OE) 'mighty warrior'. Also Ranald, Roald, Ronan, Ronel, Ronello, Roone   42, 53

Rooney (Irish) 'red-haired'   117

Rory (Irish) 'red king'. Also Ruairi   42

Ross (Lat) 'rose', or Scots 'headland'. Also Rocario   40

Rowan (ON) 'rowan-tree'   53, 105, 117

Roy (OF) 'king'   42

Rudolph (OG) 'fame-wolf'. Also Rodolfo, Rodolph, Rolf, Rudolf, Rudy   10

Rudyard (OE) 'from the red compound'. Also Rudd   81

Rufus (Lat) 'red'. Also Ruffin   53, 58, 105

Rupert (OF) 'fame-bright'   48, 74, 105

Russell (Lat) 'red'   18, 42, 106, 117

Ryan (Irish) 'little king'. Also Ryen   40

S

Sacheverell (Fr) 'without leather'   53

Salvatore (Lat) 'saviour'. Also Salvador   65

Samuel (Heb) 'name of God'. Also Sam   38, 76, 105

Sampson (Heb) 'child of sun'. Also Samson   102, 113, 116, 126, 130

Saul (Heb) 'asked-for'. Also Sol

Saxon (OG) 'sword'   53, 74, 102

Scott (OE) 'Scottish'   40, 102

Seamus (Heb) 'supplanter'   46, 61

Sean (Heb) 'Jehovah has favoured'

Sebastian (Lat) 'venerable'. Also Bastian   46, 81, 105

Secundus (Lat) 'the second'. Also Secundo   109
Sefton (OE) 'rush-dweller'   74
Selwyn (OE) 'friend of the house'   74, 106
Seneca (Lat) 'old'
Septimus (Lat) 'seventh'   15, 110
Serle (OG) 'armour'. Also Sarilo, Serill   53
Seth (Heb) 'appointed'   44
Seton (OE) 'sea-town'
Sewal (OE) 'victorious strength'. Also Sewell
Sextus (Lat) 'the sixth'   110
Shane (Heb) 'Jehovah has favoured'   40
Shaun (Heb) 'Jehovah has favoured'
Shaw (OE) 'from the grove'   42
Sheridan (Irish) 'wild man'   87
Sholto (Scot) 'sower'   102, 115
Sidney (Gk) 'follower of Dionysus'   18, 106
Siegfried (OG) 'victorious peace'
Sigmund (OG) 'victorious protector'. Also Sigurd   61
Silas (Lat) 'of woodland'. Also Silvain, Silvan, Silvano, Silvanus, Silverio, Silvester, Silvio, Silvius, Sylvain   44, 53, 105, 106, 126, 127
Simen (Gipsy) 'likeness'   59
Simon (Heb) 'hearkening'. Semjon, Sim, Simkin, Simm, Simeon, Simpkin, Symon, Ximines   12, 44, 46, 72, 79, 103, 105, 131
Sinclair (Fr) 'from St Clair'   113
Sior (Gk) 'farmer', the Welsh for George
Siward (OE) 'victorious protector'   6, 53, 126
Solomon (Heb) 'peaceful'. Also Salmon, Salomo, Salomon, Sol, Zol   72, 116
Somerset (OE) 'yonder place', or 'summer steading'   116
Spencer (OF) 'steward'   18
Stacy (Gk) 'resurrection'
Stanley (OE) 'stony meadow'   54
Stephen (Gk) 'crown'. Also Esteban, Estien, Estvan, Etiennes, Stavros, Stefan, Stefano, Stepan, Stephan,

Stephanus, Stepka, Stevan, Steven   42, 45, 62, 65, 79, 103

Stiggur (Gipsy) 'gate'   59

Stinson (OE) son of stone

Storr (ON) 'great one'   102

Stuart (OE) 'steward'. Also Stewart   18, 40, 42, 103

Sven (ON) 'Swede'. Also Svarne, Svend, Swen

Swain (ON) 'boy'

Swithin (OE) 'strong'. Also Swithun   8, 53

T

Talbot (OF) 'wood-cutter'   18, 53

Tam (Heb) 'twin'   44

Tancred (OG) 'advice'   53, 74

Tarquin (Lat) the name of one of Rome's earliest tyrants, Tarquin the Proud

Tas (Gipsy) 'bird's nest'   59

Tavish (Irish) 'twin'   61

Tawno (Gipsy) 'tiny'   59

Teague (Irish) 'poet'. Also Tadgh, Taig, Teige   53, 61

Terence (Lat) 'smooth'. Also Tarrance, Terencio, Terrance, Terry, Thierry   42, 64, 76

Tertius (Lat) 'third'   109

Theodore (Gk) 'gift of God'. Also Feodor, Taddeo, Teador, Teodor, Teodoro, Tewdwr, Thaddeus, Theo, Theodor, Tudor   12, 15, 65, 72, 76, 119

Thomas (Heb) 'twin'. Also Tam, Tamas, Thom, Tom, Tomas, Tomaso, Tomasz, Tomkin, Tomlin   12, 38, 45, 62, 79, 103, 111, 132

Thor (ON) 'strength'. Thor was the Norse god of war and thunder. Also Thorald, Thordis, Thore, Thorin, Thorkell, Thorvald, Thorwald, Torald, Torre, Torvald, Turold, Tyrus   6, 53, 61, 102, 111, 117

Thurstan (ON) 'Thor's stone'   8, 53

Timon (Gk) 'honourable' 126

Timothy (Gk) 'honouring God'. Also Timofei, Timoteo 12, 72, 103

Titus (Gk) 'of the race of giants' 4, 15, 53, 81, 102, 126

Tobit (Heb) 'son of Tobias'. Also Tobin

Toby (Heb) 'God is good', short form of Tobias 48, 72, 76, 81, 105, 126

Tobbar (Gipsy) 'road' 59

Todd (OE) 'fox' 40, 76, 87

Torquil (ON) 'Thor's cauldron' 53

Trevor (Welsh) 'large village'. Also Trefor, Trevar 42

Tristan (Celt) 'clamour', or French 'sad'. Also Drystan, Triston, Tristram 48, 58, 81, 105, 127

Troy (Irish) 'infantryman', and the name of a famous city in Turkey. Also Troilus 40, 106, 126

Tybalt (OE) 'bold for the people'. Also Tibald, Tibalt 53, 105, 126

U

Ulric (OG) 'wolf-ruler'. Also Alaric 87

Ultimo (Lat) 'the last' 111

Urban (Lat) 'from the city'. Also Urbano 72

V

Valentine (Lat) 'healthy'. Also Valentin, Valentino 58, 75, 126

Valerian (Lat) 'strong' 53

Vasilis (Gk) 'lordly'

Vassily (Slav) 'steadfast protector'

Vaughan (Welsh) 'small'

Vernon (Lat) 'springlike' 115

Victor (Lat) 'victorious'. Also Vic, Vittorio 40, 42, 65

Vidal (Lat) 'vital'   112, 115

Vincent (Lat) 'conquering'. Also Vincenz, Vincenzo, Vince   40, 42, 102

Virgil (Lat) 'staff-bearer'

Vito (Lat) 'alive'. Also Vitalis, Vitas, Vitus   53, 76, 112, 115

Vivian (Lat) 'lively'   58, 74, 112, 115

Vladimir (Slav) 'powerful prince'   62

W

Wallace (OE) 'Welshman'   18

Walter (OG) 'powerful warrior'   10, 17, 45, 72, 132

Warren (OG) 'defender'   40

Wayne (OE) 'wagon'   40, 106

Wen (Gipsy) 'winter'   59

Wesh (Gipsy) 'woods'   59

Wesley (OE) 'western meadow'

Wilfred (OE) 'wish for peace'. Also Wilfrid, Wilfried, Wilfredo   17, 72

William (OG) 'helmet of resolution'. Also Bill, Guillaume, Guillermo, Guillim, Guillot, Gwylim, Liam, Vilmos, Wilem, Wilhelm, Willard, Willem, Wilmar, Wilmot   10, 38, 45, 63, 64, 74, 76, 79, 103, 128, 132

Winston (OE) 'friendly town'   72

Wolf (OG) 'wolf'. Also Wulf, Wulfram   102

Wulfric (OE) 'wolf-rule'   53

Wulfstan (OE) 'wolf-stone'   53

Wystan (OE) 'battle-stone'   53, 72

X

Xavier (Arab) 'bright'. Also Javier

Y

Yarb (Gipsy) 'scented herb'   59
Yule (OE) 'Christmas-born'. Also Yul   118

Z

Zack A derivative of Isaac. Also Zak   44, 76